High-Conflict Parenting Post-Separation

High-Conflict Parenting Post-Separation: The Making and Breaking of Family Ties describes an innovative approach for families where children are caught up in their parents' acrimonious relationship – before, during and after formal legal proceedings have been initiated and concluded.

This first book in a brand-new series by researchers and clinicians at the Anna Freud National Centre for Children and Families (AFNCCF) outlines a model of therapeutic work which involves children, their parents and the wider family and social network. The aim is to protect children from conflict between their parents and thus enable them to have healthy relationships across both 'sides' of their family network.

High-Conflict Parenting Post-Separation is written for professionals who work with high-conflict families – be that psychologists, psychiatrists, child and adult psychotherapists, family therapists, social workers, children's guardians and legal professionals including solicitors and mediators, as well as students and trainees in all these different disciplines. The book should also be of considerable interest for parents who struggle with post-separation issues that involve their children.

Prof. Dr Eia Asen, MD, FRCPsych, is a consultant child, adolescent and adult psychiatrist who has worked for 40 years in the NHS. For many years he was the clinical director of the Marlborough Family Service, a systemically oriented child, adolescent and family mental health service based in the centre of London. Since 2013 he has been working as a psychiatrist and family therapist at the Anna Freud National Centre for Children and Families and he also holds the position of Visiting Professor at University College London. He has published ten books and many scientific papers and frequently teaches in Europe, the USA and Asia.

Dr Emma Morris, DClinPsy, is a Consultant Clinical Psychologist who worked at the Marlborough Family Service with Prof. Asen for ten years before moving to the Anna Freud National Centre for Children and Families in 2014. In her current role as Senior Clinician for the Specialist Trauma and Maltreatment Service at the Centre she leads on several projects including a busy clinical service for contact and residence cases. She has published research in peer-reviewed journals and regularly provides teaching and consultation in academic and professional settings both in the UK and Europe.

The Anna Freud National Centre for Children and Families: Best Practice

Series Editors: Chloe Campbell & Elizabeth Allison

An innovative new series of books written by clinicians and researchers at the Anna Freud National Centre for Children and Families on key aspects of meeting the challenges to child and adolescent mental health we currently face. Ranging from clinical practice – with titles focussing on infancy through to adolescence – to research and implementation issues around finding out what works for whom, and how to put what works into practice, each book will provide an authoritative and cutting-edge account of current best practice. Clearly and concisely written, the books in this series will be essential reading for professionals concerned with child mental health – psychologists, mental health workers, counsellors and psychotherapists, as well as teachers, youth workers and anyone interested in the education and care sectors.

For more information about this series please visit: www.routledge.com/The-Anna-Freud-National-Centre-for-Children-and-Families/book-series/AFNCCFBP

High-Conflict Parenting Post-Separation

The Making and Breaking of Family Ties

Eia Asen and Emma Morris

Routledge
Taylor & Francis Group

LONDON AND NEW YORK

First published 2020
by Routledge
2 Park Square, Milton Park, Abingdon, Oxon OX14 4RN

and by Routledge
52 Vanderbilt Avenue, New York, NY 10017

Routledge is an imprint of the Taylor & Francis Group, an informa business

British Library Cataloguing-in-Publication Data
A catalogue record for this book is available from the British Library

Library of Congress Cataloging-in-Publication Data
A catalog record has been requested for this book

ISBN: 978-1-138-60358-5 (hbk)
ISBN: 978-1-138-60360-8 (pbk)
ISBN: 978-0-429-46895-7 (ebk)

Typeset in Times New Roman
by Swales & Willis, Exeter, Devon, UK

Contents

Acknowledgements

We have had many discussions with other practitioners in the field. We have also reviewed the existing literature extensively and benefitted from the expertise, concepts and interventions devised by colleagues working in different settings and countries with high-conflict families post-separation. We have tried to reference all the sources that have informed our model, but we are also aware that we may have left out some important influences and inspirations – and we apologize for any omissions. Above all, we are most grateful to all the colleagues working with us over the years in the court team at the Marlborough Family Service in London and the CRD team at the Anna Freud National Centre for Children and Families – Jane Dutton, Judy Henry, Joanne Jackson and Shadi Shahnavaz. In addition we want to thank Mrs Gill Gorell Barnes and Lord Justice Peter Jackson for many helpful conversations and suggestions. We are also grateful to Chloe Campbell and Liz Allison for their most professional editorial assistance.

The case examples provided throughout this book are fictional and based on the authors' experience of typical scenarios encountered when working with high-conflict separated parents and their children.

Introduction

The book describes assessment and therapeutic work with high-conflict separated parents – before, during and after formal legal proceedings have been initiated and concluded. It is written for professionals who work with high-conflict parental separation – be that psychologists, psychiatrists, child and adult psychotherapists, family therapists, social workers, children's guardians and legal professionals including solicitors and mediators, as well as students and trainees in all these different disciplines. The book should also interest parents who struggle with post-separation issues involving their children.

The Family Ties approach has been developed over the past 20 years and much of the work has involved family courts where often decisions are made with regard to where children should live (residence/custody) and how much time (contact/visitation) they should spend with each parent. Family Ties aims to assist the outcome of parental post-separation battles when dependent children become entangled in their parents' chronic acrimonious relationship. Not infrequently they feel the need to side with one parent against the other and, after their parents' physical separation, their relationship with the parent they do not live with is often adversely affected. When inter-parental conflicts persist or further escalate post-separation, children can, in more extreme cases, totally refuse to have any form of direct or indirect contact with the other parent. It is at this stage that lawyers – and eventually also courts – become involved in order to find resolution.

Various approaches have been developed for helping children from high-conflict families so that they can develop and/or sustain good and appropriate relationships with both their parents in order to support and protect their psychosocial development. These approaches have different conceptual foundations and assumptions. Various terms, such as 'parental alienation', 'estrangement' and 'justifiable rejection', have been introduced and there has been considerable debate about their usefulness and limitations. It is our view that these descriptions are one-dimensional if not over-simplistic. They can evoke unhelpful victim–perpetrator scenarios where one parent 'alienates' the child(ren) from the other parent, with the 'alienated parent' and the child(ren) being the victims. Dynamics in high-conflict families and the positions children find themselves in are usually much more complex, not least because children have minds of their own, even if these can be influenced. It is for this reason that we have developed a model for understanding and working with high-conflict families – Family Ties – enabling practitioners to design interventions with a primary focus on the child's welfare, as opposed to apportioning blame to one or both parents.

Family Ties aims to change family dynamics by strengthening positive family ties and relationships as well as freeing children from being restricted by unhealthy family ties. Children can, metaphorically speaking, be 'tied in knots' by loyalty conflicts and be constrained and even controlled by the opposing demands, real or imagined, of their parents and members of their respective families of origin. Family ties can have both positive and negative aspects: on the one hand, they keep up connections and help family members with their attachments, feeling contained and secure. On the other hand, family ties can constrict, restrain and constrain and, in the context of high-conflict families post-separation, they can make children feel that they are 'chained' to one of their parents at the expense of the other.

Family Ties integrates the concepts of attachment and mentalizing in a systemic framework (see Chapter 2) – the family and the various 'systems' it is part of, such as the extended family and the wider social and cultural setting. The paramount focus is on the best interests and well-being of the child(ren) and the quality of 'fit' between parenting capacity and the child's psychosocial functioning and developmental needs. The first chapter sets out the family context within which children and their parents find themselves when they separate and when they cannot agree where the children should live and how much time they should spend with each parent. The conceptual framework and model of the Family Ties approach are described in Chapter 2. The legal contexts and issues that arise when chronic litigation looms are set out in Chapter 3. Chapters 4–6 describe in some detail how to assess children, parents and family relationships so that interventions can be planned. Chapter 7 focuses on how to assist children and parents to re-establish and sustain a meaningful relationship with a rejected parent. Chapter 8 aims to help practitioners who engage in the often stressful work with high-conflict families post-separation, and summarizes the principles of ensuring safe and reflective practice. Chapter 9 provides suggestions for parents who want to avoid litigation and court hearings and explains how early intervention may help in this respect.

Last, not least, we would like to emphasize that before rushing into undertaking assessments and designing therapeutic interventions, it is important to allow the dust to settle when parents separate: some initial chaos is normal when a family literally falls apart and it is usually not helpful to pathologize the process of the individual members trying to find a new modus vivendi.

Chapter 1

High-conflict parenting
The family context

Case example

When Mrs B and Mr B met some 15 years ago, it was what they still refer to now as 'love at first sight'. Things went well for the first five years until baby Rahul arrived. Pregnancy and birth were both very difficult and Rahul turned out to be a rather demanding infant. Mr B had a high-pressure job and worked long hours. Mrs B, who had previously worked full time as a pharmacist, stayed at home with the baby. Both parents were stressed and exhausted and major arguments started about childcare, different expectations and cultural practices, the role of the in-laws, and more. By the time their second child, Marina, arrived two years later the parents' relationship was at an all-time low. Mrs B felt that Mr B was not the 'hands on' father he promised he would be. He was rarely at home and when he was, he was usually stressed and behaved in controlling ways towards her and the children. He showed her little affection or recognition for all the work she did in the family home. She suspected him of having an affair which he vehemently denied. Mr B, on the other hand, felt that the household was dominated by his mother-in-law who had moved close to the family home, and visited almost daily. Mrs B and her mother often criticized him and rarely consulted him about important decisions. He felt marginalized, as if his role as the father to the children was being undermined, that his views and opinions went unheard and that the children only ever wanted their mother. The atmosphere in the family home became very tense with daily arguments, initially only when the children were not present or asleep, but increasingly also in front of the children. Soon Rahul presented with frequent temper tantrums and Marina had difficulty with feeding and sleeping. Matters between the parents deteriorated further; Rahul was three years of age and Marina barely one when Mr B decided to move out of the family home. He felt that his wife no longer respected him and that he was 'not allowed' to be the father he wanted to be. Mrs B, on the other hand, felt abandoned by Mr B and took his decision to leave the family home as evidence that he was not truly committed to their family. Both agreed that Mr B could have the children stay with him every other weekend and that he could also have them stay midweek for one night. Mrs B said that she wanted to preserve the children's relationship with their father, but worried about his lack of experience caring for the children. Each time the children returned from staying with their father, the mother experienced them as not settling down and being more difficult to manage over subsequent days. After two months, Mrs B said that Marina could not continue the overnight stays with her father who protested but to no avail. Rahul now came on his own to stay with his father, but he said that he was missing his sister and his mum. Three months later, Rahul refused to spend a weekend with his father. He did not want to get ready to leave and he behaved in a clingy way towards his mother. He told her 'daddy is grumpy and he shouts'. Mrs B called Mr B and said she had tried 'literally everything' to persuade Rahul to see his father but that he was refusing to do so. For the following four months Mr B saw neither child even though every other weekend he and Mrs B spoke on the phone to plan the handover and every time it was the same: 'I have tried everything but Rahul does not want to see you – he is too old for me to force him to come and see you'. Mr B became increasingly frustrated that the children's mother was not doing more to support his relationship with their children. He shared his concerns with family friends who confronted Mrs B, accusing her of using the children to punish Mr B for leaving the family home. There were heated arguments between the parents in the street which were witnessed by the children and which, on one occasion, led to a neighbour calling the police. Mrs B said she experienced Mr B as angry and controlling – 'a bully' – and that he didn't really care about the children. Mr B, on the other hand, stated that she was 'deliberately alienating the children from me'. He instructed a solicitor and increasingly hostile letters were exchanged between the solicitors.

The case went to court a few months later and independent
social workers and other professionals became involved. By the
time Rahul was eight years of age, some ten court hearings had
taken place, with various orders being made for both children to
spend time with their father – but these seemed unenforceable.
At the point of referral to the clinic, neither child had seen nor
spoken to their father for four years. Rahul said he 'hated' his
father 'who shouted at me and Mummy' and Marina appeared to
show no interest in her father.

Parental acrimony and resulting family dynamics

The family is often referred to as a safe haven. Yet, it can also be, or
become, a major battleground. It is estimated that in the USA and UK
more than 40% of marriages end in divorce and the situation does not
appear to be all that different in many other European countries
(OECD 2018). Almost one in three children will experience a parental
divorce before the age of 16 and in about 10% of all divorce cases
there are very high levels of conflict (Bream & Buchanan 2003). High-
conflict parenting post-separation frequently leads to contact and residence disputes: serious disagreements about who should have the main
custody of the children, where and with whom they should live and
how much direct and indirect contact they should have with each
parent. These disagreements are often not limited to the two parents
but also involve extended family, friends and professional networks. In
such scenarios, children are at risk of suffering emotional harm as the
result of being exposed to and involved in their parents' problematic
conflict management and lack of resolution.

Most parents who separate are able to put their children first and
try to protect them from exposure to parental acrimony. Post-separation, they support their children's important need to have relationships with both their parents and their respective extended family
and friendship networks. However, there are also those parents who
find it impossible to set aside their conflicts and, as in the example
above, bit by bit, their children get drawn in, often eventually
taking sides. As intense feelings and even more intense responses
fuel the conflicts further, friends and wider family begin to gather
and support one or the other side and it is only a matter of time
before the widening conflict involves lawyers and other professionals. The adversarial nature of the legal system can then contribute to a further polarization. As the main adult attention becomes

focused on winning the case, the main losers are almost inevitably the children whose complex emotions and loyalty issues are no longer properly considered, obscured by the highly emotive war that is raging between the parents and members of the wider system, be that extended family, friends and even professionals.

When parental couples divorce or separate, some will already have a long history of partnership difficulties, usually also involving members of their respective families of origin prior to the divorce. Disputes can go on for many years with the adults' narratives becoming increasingly more rigid or frozen over time, often as the result of prolonged legal battles (Blow & Daniel 2002; Gorell Barnes 2005). Children are generally acutely aware of their parents' long-standing acrimony and disputes, even if their parents claim that they are protecting them from being exposed to these. As they become caught up in their parents' fights – whether directly or indirectly – children may experience conflicts of loyalty, leading to feeling the need to take a firm position, such as siding with one parent against the other. When separated parents live in different homes, children frequently begin to idealize the parent they live with and sometimes the parent they spend less time with. However, more often than not, the non-resident parent runs the risk of being side-lined, and sometimes being actively denigrated or even demonized. When such positions are not challenged or when they are deliberately or inadvertently reinforced and encouraged, they can become exaggerated. Occasionally, children may make allegations of past maltreatment by the distanced or absent parent, alleging incidents of neglect or abuse which then serve as the trigger for the resident parent to reduce or terminate contact with the non-resident parent, or insist that contact be supervised.

Parental separation can be a challenging transition which demands re-structuring and adjustment within the family and parents not infrequently enter into legal proceedings as a way of maintaining identity when former roles or position within the family are threatened (Gorell Barnes 2017), with an expectation that these will mediate the complex emotions between the former partners (Trinder et al. 2008). If in addition new partners have joined one or both parents, further complex dynamics are likely to emerge which can adversely affect the relationships children have – or have had – with one or both their parents. How children cope with their parents' separation, both in the short and long term, very much depends on their parents' ability and willingness to co-parent competently.

Parental separation and its effects on children

Parental separation normally causes strong feelings for children, ranging from distress to anxiety, sadness and anger (Kelly & Emery 2003b). More often than not, children are poorly informed by their parents about an impending separation or divorce and the reasons for it, and little is said about the long-term implications with regard to the future family structure and contact and residence issues – usually because the parents themselves are unsure of these. When one parent moves out of the family home, the remaining parent may frame the departure of the non-resident parent differently to how the latter does. As a result, children are confused as to what the 'real story' is. In the immediate aftermath of a physical separation, children are likely to see the non-residential parent less frequently and sometimes not for weeks.

It is well documented that parental tensions and acrimonious conflicts do generally have negative effects on children and their psychosocial development (Barletta & O'Mara 2006; Holmes 2013; Bernet et al. 2016; Harold & Sellers 2018), so much so that more recently DSM-5 (2013) introduced the diagnostic condition of 'child affected by parental relationship distress' (CAPRD). It is not the separation itself, but the destructive inter-parental conflict that is found to be associated with poor adjustment for children in the years that follow (Emery 1982; Kline et al. 1991), depending also on the extent to which children are drawn into the parental conflicts (Davies & Cummings 1994; Buchanan & Heiges 2001; McIntosh 2003), and whether they feel at fault for, or threatened by, their parents' acrimonious relationship (Harold et al. 2007). Whilst the emotional security of some children will be more affected than that of others, repeated and prolonged direct exposure to inter-parental conflicts and arguments carries considerable mental health risks for all children. These include anxiety and depression, as well as behavioural difficulties including aggressive and hostile behaviours (Johnston et al. 1987; Buchanan & Heiges 2001; Grych & Fincham 2001; Cummings & Davies 2002; McIntosh 2003; Harold & Murch 2005; Jenkins et al. 2005; Holt et al. 2008; Pinnell & Harold 2008), difficulties in interpersonal relationships (Bolgar et al. 1995), loyalty conflicts and cognitive dissonance (Amato & Afifi 2006) and poorer adjustment (Kline et al. 1991). Affected children are also more likely to experience future difficulties in forming and sustaining trusting relationships. When parents battle with each other, their emotional availability to their children can become significantly reduced as many of their actions and responses are organized around the ongoing conflicts rather than their children's needs. Each parent may well claim that they only want to do their best for their children, blaming the other parent and finding it difficult, if not impossible, to see the role they themselves play in feeding acrimonious family relationships. Domestic abuse not infrequently continues following parental separation, with children's contact levels with the non-resident parent becoming a central focus for abusive interactions between parents (Morrison 2015). In this scenario, children's relationships with both their parents are usually adversely affected even though the primary focus may be on the relationship with the 'alienated' parent.

The parental alienation debate

The term 'parental alienation' (Gardner 1985) refers to the unwarranted rejection of an 'alienated' parent by the child, whose alliance with the 'alienating' parent is characterized by extreme negativity towards the other parent, as the result of a 'conscious action' of one parent to oust the other parent from the love and respect of their child (Lowenstein 2007). The child is said to form a strong coalition with the resident or 'preferred' parent and to reject a relationship with the other 'rejected' parent with 'no legitimate justification' (Gardner 1998). The diagnosis of 'Parental Alienation Syndrome' (PAS) (Gardner 1985) remains controversial as it suggests that the child develops a 'disorder' as a result of the deliberate or unconscious indoctrination by an 'alienating' parent, often accompanied by what may appear to be trivial, false or unsubstantiated allegations made by children against the alienated parent. Support for the notion that children can seemingly believe the false allegations that they make against the rejected parent comes from a significant body of research demonstrating that memory can easily be distorted and that 'false memories' can be implanted (Loftus 1997; Bruck & Ceci 1999; Schacter 2001; Tavris & Aronson 2007; Lilienfeld et al. 2010).

Specific parental behaviours have been found to be typically associated with parent-rejecting children of high-conflict separated parents (Baker & Darnall 2006; Baker 2007; Baker & Chambers 2011; Ben-Ami & Baker 2012). Darnall (1998) has summarized three categories of 'alienating parents': (1) 'Naïve alienators' who are passive about the relationship with the other parent and occasionally say or do something that may contribute to what can develop into alienating processes. (2) 'Active alienators', who know what they are doing is wrong but, in an effort to cope with personal hurt and anger, 'alienate' as a result of emotional vulnerability or poor impulse control. (3) 'Obsessed alienators', who feel justified in hurting the target parent and destroying the child's relationship with that parent, rarely showing self-control or insight (Darnall 1998). Further overlapping terms and categorizations have been introduced by other practitioners in order to explain why children may seemingly side with one parent and reject the other. The term 'justifiable estrangement' (see Bala & Hebert 2016; Whitcombe 2017) has been coined to describe a child's 'understandable rejection' of an abusive or neglectful parent. 'Hybrid cases' are said to combine both 'alienation' and 'justifiable estrangement' to account for the rejection of one parent (Friedlander & Walters 2010). Other terms and concepts such as 'family member marginalization' (Scharp & Dorrance 2017) and 'counterproductive protective parenting' (Drozd & Williams Olesen 2004) or 'unfair disparagement of one parent by another' have also been used to describe the process of why a child may not see a parent. Kelly and Johnston (2001) have attempted to reformulate PAS and focus instead on the 'alienated child', detailing why and how children's relationships with their parents can be affected post-separation. The concept of 'implacable hostility' (Sturge & Glaser 2000) represents another attempt to describe the intense and unchanging level of hostility which is often two-way between the resident and non-resident parents. This latter concept has its limitations in that it may be taken to imply that the situation cannot be improved, possibly discouraging practitioners from attempting change-promoting interventions.

There has been much debate on whether or not parental alienation actually exists as a syndrome or not (see, for example, Andre 2004; Bernet et al. 2010; Rand 2011; Gottlieb 2012; Baker et al. 2016; Cantwell 2018). In our view the concept of 'alienation' has some merits, but it also has its limitations in that it postulates a one-directional linear and causal process rather than taking full account of the complex processes that can lead to children becoming drawn into their parents' acrimonious relationships and result in the rejection of one of their parents. Whilst we recognize that in very extreme cases one parent may be the major driving force responsible for undermining a child's relationship with the other parent, in most cases there are broader and more complex dynamics – 'misaligned child triangulation' and 'alienating processes' – at play, requiring a more nuanced understanding and formulation.

Fidler and Bala (2010) cite numerous studies indicating the possible negative effects of alienating processes on children. These may include

- Poor reality testing
- Illogical cognitive operations
- Simplistic and rigid information processing
- Inaccurate or distorted interpersonal perceptions
- Disturbed and compromised interpersonal functioning
- Self-hatred
- Low or inflated self-esteem or even omnipotence
- Pseudo-maturity
- Gender-identity problems
- Poor differentiation of self (enmeshment)
- Aggression and conduct disorders
- Disregard for social norms and authority
- Poor impulse control
- Emotional constriction, passivity or dependency
- Lack of remorse or guilt (Fidler & Bala 2010).

Retrospective qualitative studies of adults who were subjected to alienating processes in childhood are in line with these findings (Baker 2007; Verrocchio et al. 2018). Most of the affected adults reported that, while they distinctly recalled claiming during childhood that they hated or feared the rejected parent and often had negative feelings towards them, they did not want that parent to walk away from them and had secretly hoped someone would realize that they did not mean what they said. These are by no means new findings as, almost three decades ago, Clawar and Rivlin (1991) reported that 80% of their sample of children conveyed that they wanted alienating processes to be detected and stopped.

Family Ties and child triangulation processes

The Family Ties model postulates that it is the process of children becoming drawn – 'triangulated' – into persisting parental conflicts that accounts for the particular relationships one finds in high-conflict families post-separation. Different from the psychoanalytic concept of 'early triangulation' (Abelin 1975), in the systemic field triangulation processes usually refer to children becoming involved in adult disputes and forming problematic alliances with one of their parents against the other. Bowen (1966), for example, introduced the term 'pathological triangulation': a cross-generational coalition, with one parent using the child as a confidante and excluding and demeaning the other parent. The 'perverse triangle' (Haley 1967) similarly alludes to the process of one parent co-opting their child in a covert collusion to isolate the other parent; this places the child in a 'no win' situation, as complying with one parent means losing the love of the other parent. Selvini Palazzoli et al. (1990) outlined specific 'family games' which can trap children and young persons and cause severe psychological disorder. Boszormenyi-Nagy and Spark (1973) depicted the 'invisible loyalties' and 'role corruption' children suffer in these scenarios, often leading to what Minuchin (1974) termed 'dysfunctional power hierarchies' and 'enmeshed' parent–child relationships. In these scenarios children are at an increased risk of being 'adultified', 'parentified' and/or 'infantilized' (Garber 2011b).

Child triangulation involves three different and overlapping distancing and alienating processes (see Figure 1.1). The distancing of one parent from the child is one such process and can be linked to the extent to which a parent supports the child's ongoing relationship with the other parent. Parents who despite any feelings of anger or upset they may have towards the other parent, nevertheless wholeheartedly support their child's relationship with the other parent, are at one end of the continuum. On the same continuum one can also

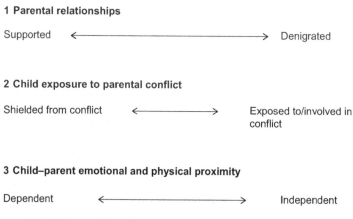

1 Parental relationships

Supported   ←——————————————→   Denigrated

2 Child exposure to parental conflict

Shielded from conflict   ←—————→   Exposed to/involved in conflict

3 Child–parent emotional and physical proximity

Dependent   ←—————————→   Independent

Figure 1.1 Child triangulation processes

encounter indirect and inadvertent undermining of the relationship and, at the very other end of the spectrum, there is the deliberate, continuous and consistent undermining of the child's relationship with the other parent, including denigration of that parent.

A second process contributing to child triangulation is the degree of exposure and involvement of the child in the inter-parental conflicts. At one end of the spectrum children may be entirely shielded from their parents' conflicts whereas, at the other end of the continuum, they are consistently exposed to most of their parents' acrimonious interactions and often become directly involved in inter-parental disputes.

A third contributing factor to distancing and alienating processes concerns the actual physical and emotional proximity between a child and parent. One end of the spectrum marks a very close and dependent relationship between a child and parent, whereas at the other end of the continuum there is a complete independence of the child from the parent. The optimum position for a child's relationship with a parent along this spectrum depends on many factors, such as age, developmental stage, societal norms as well as the family's unique situational, social and cultural circumstances. When a child has been triangulated by their parents, the degree of proximity to the resident parent is often closer, and that to the non-resident parent further than would be optimal for their healthy development.

In cases where a child has actually experienced significant abuse or neglect from a parent, some degree of physical and/or emotional distance from that parent is not only understandable, but it is also usually in the child's best interest – especially if there is a continued real risk of further emotional or physical harm. This dynamic is different from being triangulated into a highly conflictual inter-parental relationship as we only speak about 'child triangulation processes' when the emotional and/or physical distancing of a child from one parent is the result of that relationship being undermined by the other parent and/or the result of that child being exposed to inter-parental conflict rather than as a result of the harm that child has experienced in the distanced parent's care.

The evolving dynamics and processes can perhaps be best disentangled and addressed when trying to understand the views and respective stances of each member of the triangle: the parent with whom the child spends most time (referred to from here on as the 'closer parent'); the parent the child spends less or no time with (the 'distanced parent'); and the affected child.

The concepts of 'closer' and 'distanced' parents

The closer parent can contribute to child triangulation processes by, for example, being critical or over-critical of how the other parent is treating or has treated the child. This may lead the closer parent to genuinely believe – and without any malice – that the relationship between the child and the other parent needs to be limited or stopped altogether, so as to protect the child from any feared harm or from inadequate or bad parenting. Such concerns can become amplified when parents have difficulties in differentiating their own thoughts and feeling states (for example of anger and/or anxiety) from those of their child. In the absence of a capacity to do this, the parent is likely to find it very difficult to support the child's relationship with the other parent, thereby increasing the distance between the child and the other parent. Another dynamic that may contribute to the process of child triangulation is the closer parent's increasing reliance on the child for emotional support and/or company, which has the effect of the child possibly being drawn into that parent's 'cause' and being exposed to the parent's subjective negative feelings in relation to their ex-partner. Thus the child is indirectly exposed to the parental conflict, sees the effect it has on the closer parent and, out of loyalty to that parent and/or to protect their relationship, distances himself/herself from the other parent.

Some parents may not make negative comments about the other parent, but their own feelings of distress and/or anger mean that they find it easier not talking about that parent or are reluctant to display photos or reminders of an absent parent. This does not support the child's relationship with the distanced parent, as it makes it harder for the child to access positive memories and further creates physical and emotional distance between a child and parent. In more extreme cases, closer parents may feel aggrieved and believe that they are justified in directly and repeatedly undermining the relationship between their child and their ex-partner, and/or they may directly involve their child in the ongoing parental conflict, for example by sharing stories of domestic abuse allegedly perpetrated by the distanced parent. Parents may also plant hidden recording devices on their child to wear during contact, or coach the child to make allegations against the other parent. Members of the closer parent's family of origin and loyal friends can further contribute to child triangulation processes by reinforcing negative information and by taking sides.

The distanced parent can contribute to child triangulation processes via their response to feeling criticized by the closer parent and his/her network. This can lead them to become depressed and withdraw from the relationship with their child, who is left with feelings of anger, guilt and abandonment. Alternatively, the distanced parent may respond with criticism and hostility, without shielding the child from these strong negative feelings about the closer parent and members of his/her family, and thus indirectly exposing the child to the conflict. This can then have the effect of the child turning further away from the distanced parent, if only to protect his/her view of the closer parent. Another dynamic contributing to child triangulation processes can be the distanced parent's angry or dejected responses to their child's apparent withdrawal from their relationship. This may in turn lead to painful feelings in the child, such as anxiety, rejection or guilt, which they try to minimize or avoid by distancing themselves further from that parent. In some cases, there is a denial of poor and neglectful past parenting by the distanced parent and/or denial of incidents of physical abuse or inappropriate behaviours. Where it is documented and established that these behaviours actually took place, such denials disqualify the child's accounts of past events, which is likely to result in further distancing. In cases where the facts about the distanced parent's behaviour are disputed, such denial places the child in the difficult position of having to choose between two seeming 'truths' and deciding which parent is 'right' and 'wrong'.

There are plenty of reasons why the affected child may favour one parent over the other and be reluctant or resistant to have post-separation contact with the parent they do not live with. Children may pick up on their closer parent's anxiety at the prospect of having contact with the distanced parent and can develop anxious responses themselves. In more extreme cases they may even develop an irrational fear or aversion to the non-resident parent, resembling a phobic response. This can trigger mutually escalating cycles of anxiety, panic and avoidance behaviours, as the closer parent responds to the child's anxiety and upset by becoming more protective and fretful. The closer parent is thus not able to reassure the child or to help them overcome their anxieties and develop coping strategies. The child picks up on the closer parent's preoccupations and responses, which reinforce the sense that the other parent is 'not safe'. The child's avoidant behaviour can then become an entrenched and learned response (Fidler et al. 2013; Judge & Deutsch 2017).

Another reason why children may want to limit or altogether stop their relationship with one of their parents may be past unsatisfactory or bad experiences when being cared for by that parent, or a parent's preoccupation with relationship conflict and/or parental mental health/ substance abuse issues. Memories of such experiences can become exaggerated in a child's mind when their relationship with that parent is not supported or is actively undermined by the closer parent. Children who have been exposed to parental conflict and are aware of incidents where the distanced parent treated the closer parent badly may reject the distanced parent out of loyalty to the closer parent and/or to protect their relationship with that parent. In some cases, children are exposed to verbal accounts of allegedly bad conduct of the distanced parent that, even if they are not true or are exaggerated or distorted, come to be believed in the absence of evidence to the contrary and are used as a justification for distancing.

Finally, children may also distance themselves from a parent in order to reduce painful feelings of anxiety, guilt or loss associated with having rejected that parent or with the task of managing contradictory parental narratives around their life events. Sibling pressure may be yet another contributing factor in situations when one child may be more aligned with a parent than their brother or sister, for example a child may have been favoured – or perhaps not neglected or abused – by a parent who has treated the other siblings badly. Children who have been physically, sexually and/or emotionally abused by a parent may have understandable reasons to distance themselves from the unsafe parent and naturally rely more on, and align with, the parent who is perceived as safe.

As to the parents' interactions with each other, these tend to follow one of three patterns: (1) mutual blaming; (2) blaming-blocking whereby one parent blames the other parent, who then withdraws and blocks all further communication; (3) blocking-blocking in which both parents withdraw and block communication. This places the child in the unenviable position of occupying the space *between* the parents, being used as a go-between, messenger and pawn (Van Lawick 2016). It is this in-between space where children suffer most and it is concretely experienced immediately before, during and after making the transition from one parent to the other.

Chapter 2

Family Ties
Conceptual framework and evaluation

The main objectives of Family Ties are to de-triangulate children from parental relationship conflicts and, where appropriate, to bring the distanced parent closer to the child so that the child can have 'good enough' relationships with *both* parents. This can include reinstating indirect and direct contact with a parent a child has not seen for months or years. Beyond this, therapeutic interventions aim to establish sustained relationships with both parents and a reduction in the child's exposure to parental conflict, primarily as a result of improved co-parenting. Regardless of any further progress in complex cases, a positive experience of the distanced parent challenges children's distorted memories and representations of the distanced parent and may assist in better integrating those aspects of their developing self that they associate with that parent. It also helps children to manage, and to some extent resolve, painful feelings of guilt about rejecting one of their parents, as well as any feelings they may have regarding the perceived or actual abandonment by the distanced parent.

A number of different approaches to improve the outcomes for children affected by alienating processes have been developed over the years (Gardner 2001; Everett 2006; Lowenstein 2006; Major 2006; Lebow & Rekart 2007; DeJong & Davies 2012; Gottlieb 2012; Baker & Sauber 2013; Fidler et al. 2013; Woodall & Woodall 2017; Hertzmann et al. 2016; Hertzmann et al. 2017) and they contain many helpful concepts and intervention techniques. A systemic family therapy approach to working with triangulated children has been adopted by some experts in the field and the systemic components of Family Ties have many of the characteristics of what Lebow (2003) describes as 'multi-level systemic therapy'.

The additional focus on mentalizing – thinking about the mental states of self and others – distinguishes the Family Ties approach from other models of working with high-conflict separated parents. It has been developed over the past two decades in London, using a multi-disciplinary team approach in both the NHS and in a charity setting, the Anna Freud National Centre for Children and Families. It combines systemic and mentalization-based concepts and also makes use of cognitive, behavioural and psychoeducational frameworks and interventions.

Systemic frameworks

In the Family Ties approach the family is conceptualized as a system within a larger system: the immediate and the wider family, placed within its social and cultural settings (Ackerman 1967; Bowen 1978). The family itself can be viewed as a system with different parts – the family members – who behave according to a set of explicit and implicit rules which have developed over time and sometimes over generations, governing their relationships and communications (Watzlawick et al. 1967). These rules are part of, and can also contribute to, the presenting problems which, in high-conflict families, are characterized by inter-parental acrimony and its adverse effects on children's emotions and behaviours. During assessment and therapeutic work a family's rules and patterns can be discovered or uncovered and they can be challenged and modified, so much so that new interactions between family members can emerge. Furthermore, in the systemic approach the relationships between family members and the wider system are also under scrutiny and these include, apart from each parent's social network, the professional network which gathers around the entrenched parental relationship, as well as the legal system which is over time recruited to play a major part in the inter-parental conflicts.

The work of structural and strategic family therapists (Haley 1963; Minuchin 1974) and their interest in what they termed 'dysfunctional' hierarchies between the generations or inadequate boundaries between parents and their children, is of particular relevance when assessing high-conflict families. Another major influence on the Family Ties approach is the exploration of the effects of family members' behaviours and beliefs on each other, with the use of circular and reflexive questions (Selvini Palazzoli et al. 1980; Cecchin 1987). Narrative therapists also inspired the Family Ties approach as they focus on the narratives in which children have their experience 'storied' by others, and above all by their parents. These narratives may not be altogether congruent with the child's own perception of 'reality' – for example, their actual experiences of a distanced parent might contradict the dominant narrative (White & Epston 1990) and then be experienced as problematic.

Attachment theory

Another theoretical framework informing the Family Ties approach is attachment theory, originally developed by John Bowlby (1953). Bowlby postulated the existence of a universal human need to form close affectional bonds. Attachment can be viewed as a biological and evolutionary system, designed to protect us from predators and other dangers. It is an open bio-psycho-social homeostatic system, regulating emotional experience and physiological arousal. If one wanted to ascribe a goal to the attachment system, or if one believes that it was designed for a purpose, then it is to feel safe. We are not born with the capacity to regulate our own emotional reactions, but this capacity develops via the regulatory system that evolves when the caregivers understand and respond to the infant's signals which are the expression of the infant's own inner states. The infant learns in this way that the caregivers can influence how they feel. If the infant is in a state of high – and seemingly uncontrollable – arousal, like being frightened, they will come to behave in a way that brings about physical proximity to a caregiver with the aim of being protected, soothed and calmed. How and when attachment behaviours are activated depends very much on an individual's evaluation of a range of environmental signals and how these trigger feelings of security or insecurity, safety or fearfulness.

Attachment theory holds that infants are born with a repertoire of biologically based behaviours which they employ in order to elicit the attention of and closeness to their primary caregivers at times of need. They do so by, for example, crying or clinging behaviours, or by smiling and making endearing sounds. These attachment seeking actions are usually responded to and reciprocated by the primary caregivers – like holding, touching or soothing the baby – and these responses strengthen the infant's attachment behaviours towards the caregivers. Affect attunement, or 'empathic responsiveness', describes a circular process occurring between children and their primary caregivers. It involves the caregivers' ability to perceive the child's affect and to respond in ways that match the child's behaviour and underlying affect, leading to the child perceiving the caregivers' corresponding behaviours as a response to their own affect state (Stern 1985). Being responsive to the child's needs in infancy establishes a sense of security which benefits the developing child.

For Bowlby (1969/1982) the primary attachment figure for an infant tended to be the mother and for a number of decades the mother-infant unit remained the focus of research and theory, mostly to the exclusion of other significant family members, in particular fathers but also siblings and grandparents. Since then the attachment paradigm has been broadened to include fathers and other carers in the child's network, but there still tends to be a common bias of focusing primarily on the mother-child dyad. Gorell Barnes (2017) highlights that, rather than relating child deprivation primarily to the absence of the mother, attachment theory needs to be recast in terms of 'systems of reliable relationships' that are available to an infant or child and the damage that may occur to normal development when these break down. Indeed, there are significant differences with regard to who and how families meet a child's needs across cultures. In some cultures it is more typical for child care to be a combined job of a number of significant persons of the child's network, rather than exclusively the 'job' of one or two people, as exemplified by the African proverb that 'it takes a village to raise a child'. How people care for and are attached to one another is shaped by – and embedded in – culturally patterned practices and child rearing and related interactions are formed within the family's cultural context. Dominant narratives, for example around gender roles, need to be unpicked in each case if we are to understand who is doing what for the child in order to meet their attachment needs. Furthermore, patterns of parenting have changed over time, with new ones emerging, for example with the increasing number of families where parents are in same-sex relationships. Hence, the primary attachment figure can be any person who has a significant, reliable, consistent and established role in meeting the attachment needs of a child.

Internal working models

During infancy and early childhood the organization of an individual's attachment system is reflected in their behaviour. As infants develop, the type of caregiving they receive informs the formation of cognitive structures with respect to relationships. Over time, the child's experience of caregiver responsiveness and sensitivity are internalized as 'Internal Working Models' (IWMs): a set of conscious and unconscious beliefs and expectations about relationships which are activated during times of stress and guide the individual's attention, cognition and behaviour (Bretherton 1987). Repeated experiences with the primary caregiver(s) are over time aggregated into the representational system of IWMs – and they provide prototypes for functioning in later relationships. For example, positive experiences of being comforted when upset or scared will allow an individual to turn to other people for help if or when needed.

Mary Ainsworth (Ainsworth et al. 1978) developed laboratory-based procedures to observe IWMs in action. She demonstrated that if young children are briefly separated from their caregivers in a situation unfamiliar to them (the 'strange situation' assessment), they show distinctly different patterns of behaviour. These styles of behaviour were classified into 'secure' (in response to a generally consistent, well-attuned caregiver) and 'insecure'; the latter can be categorized as either anxious/avoidant (in response to a generally emotionally and/or physically unavailable caregiver) or anxious/resistant (in response to inconsistent care-giving). These patterns are well described in the literature (see Solomon & George 2008) and the model was further developed to include the category of 'disorganized/disoriented' attachment (Main et al. 1985). This is thought to develop in frightened/frightening caregiving situations and/or in the context of trauma and it is suggested that children classed as 'disorganized' may become controlling and hence 'organized' with age. George et al. (1999) propose that the presence of controlling behaviours in children with disorganized attachment may be an unconscious strategy which aims to keep segregated material out of consciousness, preventing the child from becoming emotionally flooded and behaviourally out of control.

Parental acrimony and changing attachment representations

It is more often than not the case that, prior to the emergence of inter-parental acrimony, children will have formed good and secure attachments to both parents. However, children's attachment behaviours can change in response to intense and prolonged parental conflict in their attempt to protect the parenting they receive. This is because children are biologically driven to maintain a relationship with their primary caregivers, a survival mechanism also observed in primates (Bowlby 1953; Harlow 1960). Yet, when exposed to inter-parental conflict, they can believe that it is undesirable or perhaps even dangerous to show love for *both* parents, including for the one the child does not live with, as this is tantamount to betraying the parent they live with. Children in these situations can also learn that loyal behaviours are rewarded with affection, attention and even presents by the closer parent, whereas seemingly disloyal conduct is discouraged by parental irritation, punishing looks and threats of abandonment, a risk the child usually cannot take when already having 'lost' one loving and loved parent (Fidler & Bala 2010). In such scenarios children can develop a 'split' in the attachment representations they hold of each parent: the relationship with the closer parent may come to be described in heavily idealized terms, with negative experiences largely dismissed. Typically, children may say that the closer parent is 'always loving and caring' or 'never, ever cross', but may struggle to illustrate positive statements with concrete examples. The relationship with the distanced parent, on the other hand, is portrayed in derogatory terms, for example 'he never really cared for us' or 'he is a horrible man who was always mean to us'. Frequently children also get fixated on very specific, seemingly trivial, negative incidents that they say happened when they were in the presence of the distanced parent and that explain their rejection of that parent.

Thus, it is common in these scenarios for a child's attachment behaviour to be categorized as 'insecure-dismissive/avoidant' in relation to the closer parent and 'insecure-preoccupied/ambivalent' in relation to the distanced parent, with 'disorganized features' in the very severe cases. These dichotomous representations appear to be interdependent, in that the child seems to protect the caregiving they receive from their closer parent by idealizing him/her and splitting off any negative feelings, like anger and frustration, in relation to this parent and projecting these onto the distanced parent. Klein (1946) named this phenomenon 'splitting', an unconscious process to protect the primary caregiving relationship(s) by shielding the child from feelings of ambivalence, conflict and guilt. The pervasiveness of this seeming defence mechanism is a function of the level and type of child triangulation processes that are in operation. A child's unconscious need to use such a mechanism may be reduced if their attachment needs are met by a system of reliable relationships, rather than by merely one parent, especially in cases where the extended family and friendship network is not strongly aligned with the closer parent. The mechanism of splitting does, at least in part, explain why there often seems to be a striking lack of ambivalence or empathy on the part of the child about the loss of the relationship with the other parent and members of the extended family: difficult feelings and thoughts associated with this loss are split off and projected out but, importantly, are not resolved.

When little or no contact is taking place with a distanced parent, the child's internal representation of that parent can become increasingly distorted. The child may have the experience of the attachment figure not being available and therefore not being reliable. Furthermore, 'reality testing' whether the held negative beliefs are (still) justified, cannot take place. Extreme examples of this presentation include children exhibiting acute phobic responses at the mere utterance of the distanced parent's name, or at the sight of a photo or the very mention of there having to be some form of indirect or direct contact with that parent. Seemingly phobic responses of this nature tend to trigger increased caregiving behaviours by the closer parent who responds as if they need to protect the child from the other parent. Seeing their child distressed may also serve as 'evidence' of the harm the child is suffering and further confirm parental concerns, leading the closer parent to redouble their efforts to shield the child from exposure to the other parent. At the very extreme end of splitting processes is a child's attempt to altogether deny the existence of the other parent and/or literally 'delete' any memories of that parent.

Conflicting narratives and related attachment behaviours

It is usually a feature of high-conflict families post-separation that a number of different narratives co-exist with regard to family history and specific past events, above all in relation to the making and breaking of the parents' relationship. This can be most mystifying to children, but if the narrative is shaped only by the closer parent and if other perspectives and facts are omitted, children's bewilderment and confusion will be amplified. When children have only been exposed to negative narratives about the distanced parent, such as that the absent parent never loved and abandoned them, they eventually believe these themselves – even if there is, or has been, much evidence to the contrary. If they do have any positive feelings and/or memories of the absent parent, all they can do is keep them secret so as not to place any perceived burden on their closer parent.

Defensive splitting and secret-keeping can significantly disrupt the process of identity formation in children and it is associated with the development of serious mental health problems. Continued use of this unconscious defensive strategy prevents the child from integrating experiences generally and specifically in relation to both parents. Such difficulties may not become apparent until adolescence when the young person is faced with the task of self-integration as it becomes less possible for them to compartmentalize different areas of experience. When children and particularly adolescents attempt to 'delete' one of their parents from their lives, they also delete or disown those aspects and personality characteristics that they have inherited from that very parent. If children hold onto the view that there is nothing good about *one* of their parents, then it can cause them to seek to get rid of the seemingly 'alien' parts of the rejected or demonized parent they see in themselves. In extreme cases this can take the form of self-harm, like wanting to 'cut out' (with razor blades or knives) or 'drown' (with the help of alcohol and drugs) these seemingly unwanted or possibly even despised aspects which have become part of their 'self' (Farber 2008; Roussow 2012).

Children's experiences of realizing that they have been misled or consistently lied to about the absent parent by a primary attachment figure, usually the closer parent, is likely to have a significant impact on their attachment representation, as it questions the reliability and safety of the primary caregiver. A child's representation of attachment figure(s) forms the template that guides interactions with others and if its integrity becomes corrupted, the coherence of this template can become dismantled.

Mentalization-based concepts

Family Ties is inspired by mentalization-based concepts and interventions. Mentalizing can be defined as a form of imaginative mental activity which entails perceiving and interpreting human behaviours in terms of their intentional mental states, such as their feelings, needs, desires, beliefs, goals and reasons (Fonagy et al. 1991). This activity is for the most part preconscious. There are wide differences between individuals and families in terms of the extent to which they can, or want to, adopt a mentalizing stance or how accurate they are in doing this when they make assumptions about the internal states of others or themselves.

Attachment lays the foundation for learning about the human mind: it is the context within which mentalizing emerges and it usually develops in the relationship with the primary caregivers. Infants and young children attempt to understand their own internal experiences as well as the actions of those closest to them; they are trying to make sense of what is in their own mind and in the minds of their parents, siblings, grandparents and significant others, and how these are connected with one another. Mentalizing is a bi-directional social process (Fonagy & Target 1997): it develops in the context of interactions with others, and its quality in relation to understanding others is influenced by how well those around us mentalize. The family is the natural context of attachment relationships in which one can learn about minds. In fact, it would seem that there is a positive association between mentalizing ability and security of attachment (Fonagy et al. 2002; Slade et al. 2005). Infants and small children develop an idea of their own mind by experiencing another mind – like the mother's – who has 'my mind in her mind'. This process happens via micro-interactions whereby the primary caregiver naturally imitates the mental states of the infant, but labels them as 'not mine, but yours' to her child, by using voice tone, or facial expressions that are congruent and 'marked' (Fonagy et al. 2002). This experience of being mentalized is internalized, enabling the child to develop their own capacity for empathizing and better engaging in interactive social processes (Sharp & Fonagy 2008). The relationship between attachment and mentalizing is also bi-directional, if not circular: mentalizing difficulties are likely to adversely affect attachment relationships, and a poor attachment relationship – the experience of not being sensitively responded to – undermines the natural development of the capacity to mentalize (Kelly et al. 2005).

Employing a mentalizing approach when assessing and intervening with high-conflict families implies strengthening any of the above components and actively blocking non-mentalizing interactions and communications. The latter are recognizable when, for example, parents are unaware of the impact their actions have on their child or each other, or when they are always certain about the correctness of their views, or when they cannot accept responsibility for their actions. In other words, the general under-development or context-specific breakdown of parental mentalizing will lead clinicians to consider interventions to kick-start effective mentalizing again (Asen & Fonagy 2012b).

Family Ties makes the assumption that fundamental breakdowns in mentalizing processes feed child triangulation processes and render parents unable – sometimes temporarily, sometimes chronically – to focus on their children's complex and fluctuating states of mind, as well as on their own mental states. Mentalization-based therapies with individuals (Bateman & Fonagy 2012) and families (Asen & Fonagy 2012a) aim to restore a mentalizing stance in parents and children – as well as in members of the wider family and professionals' network.

Cognitive, behavioural and psychoeducational frameworks

Family Ties also draws on cognitive and behavioural theory and practice. For example, in cases where there has been no contact between a child and one of their parents for a significant amount of time and the child has developed an irrational aversive reaction to the prospect of contact, desensitization and graded exposure to 'the feared object', i.e. the distanced parent, alongside preparatory work with the whole family takes place (see Chapter 7). Behavioural intervention of this kind provides the opportunity to challenge distorted cognitions via direct 'live' experience. As with all desensitization and graded exposure programmes, the aim is to maintain the exposure until the child's expressed anxiety has reduced, otherwise the association between fear and the object is merely reinforced (White 1999; Vidair & Rynn 2010). Re-introduction programmes that are committed to moving at the child's pace can place inappropriate responsibility and burden on the child, who may maintain an inappropriate level of control and is faced with a painful loyalty conflict. However, depending on the severity or chronicity of the case, direct re-introduction can send children into a blind panic and their behaviour can become entirely ruled by the attachment system kicking in, resulting in clinging to the closer parent or, in more extreme cases, wetting themselves or running out of a building into the middle of a street. In this state, their minds become entirely inaccessible to any form of rational challenges or negotiation and the cycle of 'fear' can become reinforced. Thus, the Family Ties approach involves exposure at a pace and rate that is appropriate to the case, as informed by the practitioners and the family.

Some psychoeducational interventions are also employed to varying degrees in the Family Ties approach. As the term suggests, these interventions combine education with directive counseling on a range of mental health and child developmental issues. Parents can, for example, be informed by the practitioner about the likely psychological difficulties that can arise for children if they attempt to 'delete' one of their parents from their minds, or if they feel that all personality features and actions of the distanced parent are negative. Practitioners can provide parents with information about the increased vulnerability to emotional, behavioural and social problems that children are likely to develop when they are chronically exposed to interparental hostility. Furthermore, practitioners can explain to parents that the normal developmental trajectory for children includes a gradual process of separation and individuation and that this is a healthy and normal development. It can also be clarified that throughout childhood there are likely to be times when most children may favour one parent over the other and that alliances may shift – all signs of normal developmental processes. High-conflict parents who have had past experiences of contact breakdown can sometimes find this information hard to accept. They may need help to understand that children's changing attitudes and behaviours may need to be seen as normal and understandable, and do not necessarily constitute evidence that there is something wrong with the child–parent relationship, or that the child is being negatively influenced by one of the parents.

Key assumptions of Family Ties

The Family Ties approach makes a number of key assumptions:

1. Some form of safe contact with the non-resident parent is almost always in a child's best interests.
2. Children usually develop loyalty to the closer parent as their primary attachment figure. This can be amplified by child triangulation processes when, for example, the relationship with the distanced parent is not protected or is in some way denigrated, and/or when the child is exposed to the parental conflict, and/or when physical or psychological distance extends over time.
3. Practitioners cannot make a relationship happen on behalf of the parents; their role is to support the parents and their network to improve child–parent relationships and, when there has been no contact between a child and one of their parents, to facilitate this.

4. Therapeutic interventions have to meet the child's needs, not the parent's – the overarching aim is to provide the child with the opportunity to have the best relationship possible with both parents given the specific individual circumstances.
5. Interventions addressing the wider family system are required in order to effect sustainable change.

Figure 2.1 schematically represents the major components of this work. The parents are supported by the practitioner to mentalize their child and the impact of parental acrimony, both on the child, their ex-partner and themselves. This includes helping parents to understand the harmful effects of triangulation processes. The work also involves providing parents with the skills to manage their child's resistance to having contact with the distanced parent. Other aspects of the approach comprise the co-construction of a coherent narrative about why the re-introduction of contact (where appropriate) – and about

Figure 2.1 Overview of the model

family life events more generally – is so important to repair the contradictions in children's understanding of complex situations.

Key changes connected with this process and the interventions' theoretical underpinnings include:

1. A change in the child's distorted representation of the non-resident parent via direct experience of that parent alongside the establishment of a supportive narrative
2. A reduction in the child's need to hold a polarized position through the establishment of a more coherent family narrative and improvements in parental communication and mentalizing capacities
3. A reduction in child triangulation processes, and changes to patterns and feedback loops within the child's system that support these processes.

Research findings

Whilst there is a large evidence base for the effectiveness of systemic as well as cognitive-behavioural interventions and mounting evidence for the effectiveness of mentalization-based approaches, the specific evidence for therapeutic interventions addressing high-conflict families and children caught up in parental disputes is only gradually emerging. There is general agreement that a family approach which includes all members, alongside appropriate legal interventions, should be tried first (Lowenstein 1998; Friedlander & Walters 2010; Sullivan et al. 2010; Warshak 2010; Toren et al. 2013; Reay 2015). In cases of severe triangulation processes it is generally thought that traditional family therapy approaches are likely to be ineffective and may even cause further damage (Warshak 2010; Reay 2015). In such cases, interventions should be tailored to meet the specific needs of the families (Johnston & Goldman 2010). Following a systematic review of the literature on best practice in cases presenting with 'parental alienation', Templer et al. (2017) propose that interventions need to be ordered by the court and that non-compliance with court orders needs to be sanctioned, including considering a change in residence (custody) in favour of the 'targeted' (distanced) parent. They identified ten studies where parental alienation was a major factor. In most of these there were no clear or defined outcome measures; none of the studies were prospective or used a matched control group and the data analyses were retrospective using only descriptive statistics. Only one study (Toren et al. 2013) included both a treatment and a control group. However, the treatment allocation was not described, the sample size was small and there were some drop-outs prior to treatment commencing. Nevertheless, based on the available research, Templer and colleagues (2017) were able to identify similarities across the approaches and formulate comprehensive recommendations for practice where child(ren) may be resisting or refusing contact with a parent in the context of alienating processes. These are summarized in Box 2.1.

Box 2.1 Key practice guidelines identified by Templer et al. (2017)

- Psychoeducation about 'parental alienation' and its consequences
- A shared aim to protect the child from harm caused by the alienation
- Therapeutic interventions that reduce the child's distress and improve
- psychological well-being
- Cognitive techniques that challenge the targeted child's distorted thinking and promote critical thinking skills
- Work to improve the alienated parent–child relationship
- Preparation of the alienating parent for an improvement in the quality of the alienated parent–child relationship and a challenge to their distorted thinking
- Conflict resolution techniques to repair the co-parenting relationship
- Establishment of healthy boundaries and communication patterns within the family.

Measuring change

A major desired outcome of Family Ties is usually a reduction in the child's fearful, distressed and rejecting/avoidant behaviours in relation to the distanced parent. This can be measured by responses to simple questions such as: 'Is the child able to be in the company of the parent for an extended period of time without feeling distress?' Three possible outcomes can be recorded: a) no distress, b) reduced distress, or c) no change. Beyond this one can evaluate the quality and frequency of contact: 'Is the child able to interact with the parent? What is the quality of this interaction and is it improving over time?' There are various measurable indicators of improvement in the quality of the contact, such as increased eye contact, better reciprocity, increasing range of affect and growing playfulness. With regard to re-assessing attachment, an indication that the child holds a less idealized picture of the closer parent and a less derogatory picture of the distanced parent can be evidence that there is less splitting taking place. The child may present with more balanced representations of both parents when asked about the relationship or being observed during play (see Chapter 4). When observing interactions between children and their parents, in addition to noticing possibly less evidence of rejecting behaviours towards the distanced parent, the practitioner may also observe an increase in the child challenging the views of the closer parent. For example, a child who has been previously excessively compliant with the closer parent, may begin to state her own views across a range of topics which are different from those of the closer parent. Furthermore, the child may be less clingy or reluctant to separate from the closer parent when attending contact with the distanced parent. These and other signs can be indications that the child is better able to connect with positive and negative feelings in relation to both their parents – a process that is essential for healthy development. Long-term outcome data can be collected on whether contact has been sustained over time and whether this happened with or without further interventions by the court, practitioners or other services.

As far as changes in the child's behaviour and presentation are concerned, there are various measures that can be employed, including: the Strengths and Difficulties Questionnaire (Goodman 1997), Revised Childhood Anxiety and Depression Scale (Chorpita et al. 2000), Child Behaviour Checklist (Achenbach & Edelbrock 1991) and Beck Youth Inventories (Beck et al. 2001). These assessment tools can also be used to examine differences of perception between family members of a child and their seeming difficulties. It can be helpful to re-administer such measures at different points during the course of work to monitor the child's emotional well-being, as well as to explore parents' different perceptions of their child. However, the benefits of therapeutic assessment work in relation to a child's mental health are best observed in the long term. In the short term there can often be a seeming increase in emotional and/or behavioural symptoms, as a result of being exposed to loyalty conflicts and having to manage significant psychological re-adjustment.

The establishment of explicit goals, session by session, is an essential aspect of the Family Ties approach. Therapeutic intervention work does not proceed until both parents are signed up to the goal of improving, in a clearly specified and observable way, the quality of the relationship and/or contact between the child and the distanced or rejected parent. Progress towards this goal is measured and reviewed continuously. While parents are asked to commit to this goal from the outset, children are not, as it is their parents' responsibility to make the changes that will help the children to have a better relationship with the distanced or rejected parent. It is therefore the parents' task to share with the child their goal of improved relationships and/or contact with the distanced or rejected parent. Children are also asked about their goals for the work. In less entrenched high-conflict cases, children often say that they want their parents to 'argue less', or 'for it not to be so awkward', or 'to be able to see my mum without a supervisor being there'. These goals can also be used to measure progress. In the more entrenched high-conflict cases, the child's goals are more likely to be aligned with the closer parent, e.g. 'for my dad to just get the message and not to bother seeing me' or 'to stop the court proceedings and leave our mum in peace'. These and similar goals should not be challenged by the clinician, but they are brought to the attention of the resident parent, with the aim of getting the parent to take responsibility for helping the child to accept the importance of having both parents in their lives. Other goals the parents work towards include mutually agreed improvements in the co-parenting relationship, with clearly defined means of acertaining whether these have been achieved.

Chapter 3

Legal frameworks and planning the work

Chronic litigation

A frequent outcome in separating or separated high-conflict families is the 'see you in court' scenario. Legal proceedings in the family court with regard to disputes over contact and residence (as they are still colloquially known, or in American terms 'visitation' and 'custody') can become a long and drawn-out process. Typically each parent instructs their own lawyer and this introduces a new narrative that can seem quite alien to most parents. 'Legalese' is almost a language in its own right, and it can have the effect of parents feeling that their own highly personal narratives have got 'lost in translation' or been hijacked, as well as amplifying messages around blame.

The term 'chronic litigation' refers to bitterly fought cases which return repeatedly and over years to court, be that in the form of fresh applications, multiple reports and/or very lengthy and protracted proceedings. These are characterized by very high and enduring levels of parental conflict (Hunt & Trinder 2011). Numerous court orders do little to address the long-standing and seemingly implacable hostility between the parents. Apart from the toll on the affected children, these cases consume a disproportionate amount of the court's time and resources, often without a satisfactory conclusion (Kelly & Emery 2003b). Shared residence or family assistance orders are made so that the parents appear to have nothing to fight about, but the underlying disputes are usually not resolved and litigation continues, often over what appear to be trivial issues. Most orders represent only a brief pause in the litigation process rather than a permanent solution. Bringing litigation to an end often seems the only 'intervention' open to the court, highlighting the limitations of the court process in dealing with entrenched parental conflict (Asen 2010; Hunt &

Trinder 2011). Moreover, the adversarial system played out in the family court arena frequently fuels inter-parental conflicts, with each party blaming and shaming the other.

The court process

> Although this case was listed for a final hearing for care proceedings and private law proceedings, it was clear at the outset of the hearing before me that the case is not ready to be finalised. The court has thus been considering evidence upon which to make a determination of issues of fact and also to consider and decide what arrangements should be in place for the child until the determination of the proceedings. There is an Interim Care Order in place, and an agreed interim threshold document, and all the parties agree that the Interim Care Order should remain in place. The findings of fact which I have made will inform all professionals dealing with the family in the future in this difficult and distressing case, and will help them and the court, in due course, to take important decisions, and in the case of experts to prepare advice for the family or this court. This is the sixth judgment concerning this child. The first was a judgment in a final hearing in private law proceedings conducted by ...
>
> (Excerpt from a published High Court Judgment
> in a case with local authority involvement)

When parents cannot reach an agreement as to where their children should live and how often and in what circumstances they should spend time with the other parent, some form of mediation to avoid legal proceedings is often initially attempted. If this is not successful, one or both parents may issue proceedings. The court will determine at the first hearing if agreement can be reached on all the relevant issues. If this does not prove possible, the judge will have to make decisions at a final hearing, after reading and hearing all relevant evidence. The most common court order in England is a Child Arrangements Order which stipulates where the child lives and how much time the child spends with each parent, as either direct and indirect contact (see below). In cases of alleged domestic abuse, the court's task is to consider any harm which the child and the resident parent may have suffered as a consequence of past abuse or neglect, and any harm which the child and resident parent is at risk of suffering if a Child Arrangements Order is made. If the child has directly or indirectly suffered abuse or neglect from the non-resident parent, the court will only make an order for contact if it can be satisfied that the physical and emotional safety of the child and the resident parent can be secured before, during and after contact, and that the resident parent will not be subjected to further controlling or coercive behaviours by the other parent. A Specific Issue Order can stipulate, for example, what school the child should go to and what religious education the child may receive. A Prohibited Steps Order can be made to prevent any particular action by a parent, for example taking the child abroad. All court decisions are governed by the court's assessment of the child's best interests, which are paramount (i.e. to prevail over all other factors, such as parental rights).

There is a difference between 'private' law and 'public' law cases, with the latter being child care proceedings brought by social care agencies. However, there is also not infrequently an overlap between public and private law cases, especially in cases of protracted litigation where proceedings have been going on for some time and where there are grave concerns about children's welfare. It is not unusual in such cases for social care to become involved in what had started as private proceedings because of emerging child protection issues or for the court to order a special report from social services. There is further overlap as the type of child protection issues are often similar: almost all children involved in private and public law cases have suffered, or are likely to suffer, some form of emotional harm or neglect. Furthermore, a considerable number of children in both private and public law proceedings will have been exposed to domestic violence between their parents. In other words, the harm children suffer can be as serious in private as it is in public law cases, and it is therefore not surprising to find that a considerable number of children in both scenarios present with signs and symptoms suggestive of suffering from formal emotional and/or behavioural disorders.

Allegations and fact-finding hearings

It is a sad feature of many parental disputes that, to support their own cause, one parent will make allegations of abuse or neglect against the other parent. This sets in motion a process of denials and counter-accusations. Some of the allegations of maltreatment or ill-treatment may be well founded; others may be exaggerated or spurious, if not altogether invented. Some of the allegations will refer to ill-treatment – be that emotional, physical or sexual – one or both parents claim to have received at the hands of their ex-partner. Other allegations tend to involve the children and maltreatment they are alleged to have suffered. These allegations may be made by children spontaneously and/or they can be the result of parental influence.

Fact-finding court hearings are used to decide important factual issues that are in dispute between the parties or to determine whether there is any truth in specific allegations made. The most common allegations that a parent makes are that the other party has behaved in a way that was abusive, dishonest or harmful. If one parent makes allegations and the other party denies these, the judge has to consider whether there should be a fact-finding hearing. This will only be held if the allegations are likely to make a difference to the court's final decision. In preparation for a fact-finding hearing, the parent making the allegations will be asked to compile a list and the parent against whom the allegations are made will then be asked to respond to the allegations within a set timeframe. After submitting written statements in relation to the allegations, at the fact-finding hearing each parent will give oral evidence about what they believe has happened. Each party can be cross-examined about the allegations. It is for the person making the allegations to prove that they are true and the judge considers whether it is more likely than not that the allegations are true. This is the civil standard of proof, which contrasts with the criminal standard, where facts must be proved beyond reasonable doubt.

Contact issues

Contact with each parent is a right of a child and not of a parent or any other person. Unless proven otherwise, the presumption is that the involvement of both parents in the life of the child will be in the child's best interests. There is an expectation in law that where parents have separated, the parent the child lives with should allow a reasonable amount of contact with the other parent. Contact should only be restricted where this is necessary to protect the interests of the child. Contact between a parent and child can be direct, face-to-face, which can include contact during the day or overnight contact. Contact may also be indirect, such as telephone conversations, emails, letters and gifts.

It is a law in some countries, including England and Wales, that when a child is born to two parents, both have parental responsibility if both their names are entered on the birth certificate, irrespective of whether they are married or not. A parent can usually apply for parental responsibility if they do not automatically have it, but obtaining parental responsibility does not give the parent an automatic right to have contact with the child. The significance of parental responsibility is that the holder is able to participate in decisions about the child's upbringing and is treated by the outside world (schools, doctors) as having the right to have their views considered.

As to the 'rights' of children, it is generally held that all children have the need for a stable and secure place within the family. It is also held that children benefit immensely from having developmentally appropriate knowledge about their personal history, their parents and the reasons for not living with one or both of their birth parents. Children also need to understand that they can be part of more than one family and have more than one home. To meet some of these needs, a considerable body of research supports the presumption that some form of meaningful contact with the non-resident parent and grandparents is important (Amato & Rezac 1994; Seltzer & Bianchi 1988; Smyth & Ferro 2002; Kelly 2007; Westphal et al. 2015). This is particularly the case when that parent – or perhaps a grandparent – has cared for the child for a significant period of time. In these scenarios children tend to form multiple attachments of varying quality and they have to manage multiple and often seemingly contradictory emotional realities. Children who lose contact with significant family members frequently struggle with issues surrounding identity development for years; in fact it can be a lifelong process. As indirect contact by email, phone, Skype or post often breaks down and is frequently too 'unreal' for children, it is now the view of most practitioners that promoting direct face-to-face contact with the non-resident parent is desirable unless there are strong arguments to the contrary (Gilmore 2006; Trinder et al. 2008). A number of factors need to be considered, such as child safety, the child's wishes and the likely emotional impact on the child.

It is generally beneficial for children's emotional development and future mental health to re-establish and sustain good and meaningful relationships with both their parents in situations where there are no risks to the child or where any such risks can be safely managed. However, what makes the work with child triangulation cases so challenging is that the presence or absence of such risks is often contested. Furthermore, these risks may be inconsistently present over time, and judgements also need to be made about whether intervention and support can substantially reduce these risks. The main questions that need to be addressed by parents, practitioners and the court are as follows: what type of contact, with whom, where, how frequent, how long, how is it facilitated and is supervision needed?

Expert witnesses

The court may only obtain expert advice where it is 'necessary'. Once legal proceedings have been initiated in highly contested cases, a range of assessments may be requested: of the parents, the children, possibly of members of the extended family, and of each child's relationship with each parent or other primary carer(s). Above all, what is required is the assessment of each parent's ability to meet their child's physical, psychological, social and educational needs adequately. This requires individual evaluation of the child and their different needs, including each child's current mental state and emotional and social functioning. Based on the assessment, the instructed expert or expert witness – e.g. a psychologist, family therapist, independent social worker – is asked to provide opinions and recommendations in relation to very specific issues.

Medical metaphors may help to clarify the expert's tasks: making a 'diagnosis' – the expert's opinions and recommendations – so that the 'condition' can be 'treated' and appropriate actions can be taken by the court, be that by making an order or not. A major part of the assessment the expert is asked to undertake is to understand the history – aetiology and pathogenesis – of the presenting problem: the child triangulation processes and each person's current contribution to it. Furthermore, the expert needs to identify current and likely future factors that maintain and feed the harmful inter-parental dynamics.

The generally preferred approach is that a single joint expert is instructed, rather than each party selecting their own expert as the latter can have the effect of further polarizing the parties' positions, instead of bringing them closer to agreement. A single expert can also reduce each party's legal costs. When the parties cannot agree on which expert should be instructed, the court may either select the expert from a list prepared by the parties, or make its own selection. The expert's area of competence needs to be appropriate to the issues that the court has identified. It is also important that the expert has been active in the area of work or practice, has sufficient experience of the issues relevant to the specific case and is familiar with the breadth of current practice. This requires a working knowledge of the social, developmental, cultural norms and accepted legal principles applicable to the case. Where there is a question around the risk of criminal behaviour, such as sexual or violent offences, the expert must also have the relevant forensic expertise. The specialist expertise required depends on the evidence needed in a particular case and the court needs to be satisfied with the expert's qualifications, relevant experience and post-qualification training. The expert's overriding duty is to the court and this takes precedence over any obligation to the person from whom the expert has received instructions or by whom the expert is paid, so as to avoid any bias or suspicion of collusion (Asen & Schuff 2003).

Legal considerations

The court discourages unnecessary litigation and encourages parents to resolve disputes by mediation. Before proceedings begin, the applicant and, on some occasions the respondent, should attend a meeting to obtain information about the possibility of mediation (a MIAM).

When consulting a lawyer with an allegation of 'parental alienation', parents need to be aware that the lawyer will want to (Richardson 2019):

1. Obtain a clarification and precise definition of the allegation
2. Consider the evidence indicative of the allegation
3. Determine what questions need to be asked and answered so as to lay the ground for a thorough analysis of the issues
4. Make a decision as to what the consequences of the allegation, if proved, are for the child in terms of contact and residence issues
5. Present the arguments in a coherent way so as to advocate for or against what is being alleged.

The existence of Parental Alienation Syndrome is highly contested and it has been expressly rejected by the English Courts. However, the term 'parental alienation' is widely and often used indiscriminately; it is ill-defined and refers to a range of different behaviours and actions displayed by children and parents (see Chapters 1, 4 and 5). Lawyers will therefore ask their clients what precisely they mean when they make an allegation of parental alienation, in order to determine why a child may be reluctant to have a substantial relationship or any form of contact with one of their parents. There are essentially two options which lawyers consider in this scenario: (1) justified reluctance or opposition from the resident parent and/or the child due to the behaviour of the rejected parent, or (2) disproportionate and/or unjustified reluctance or opposition rooted in the unreasonable opposition of the resident parent.

In determining which of these two possibilities is likely to be true, lawyers will want to set out what is alleged not only by the instructing parent but also by the other parent. Once the allegation has been clearly defined and particularized, lawyers then consider what evidence may be available or needed to prove that the allegation is well founded or false. Four outcomes are possible: the allegation is proved, partially proved, not proved or actively false – and the ultimate arbiter of contested evidence is the court. When gathering and analysing evidence, lawyers will focus on one question at all times: is the allegation relevant or potentially relevant to the child's welfare, and if so, why? When advancing an argument, lawyers have to keep in mind the consequences arising for the child if the allegation is proved: e.g. does contact with the rejected parent need to be reinstated? Is a transfer of the child's home required? In the statements lawyers draw up jointly with their clients and when representing them in court, lawyers will need to present the arguments succinctly and coherently, advocate for or against what is alleged and argue the consequences that should follow.

The Letter of Instruction

The Letter of Instruction (LOI) sets out the nature of the evidence and outlines the circumstances of the case. It contains specific questions which need to be answered and these need to be clear, focused and kept to a manageable number. However, as an increasing number of parents represent themselves in private law cases, the process of the parties agreeing the LOI can be lengthy. A list of the most common areas for assessment identified by LOIs is shown in Box 3.1 and it can assist parents and lawyers to formulate these.

Box 3.1 List of possible LOI areas for assessment

- Psychiatric, psychological and cognitive profile of each parent
- Each parent's past and current mental health issues
- Each parent's past and current substance/alcohol misuse

- Physical and emotional availability of each parent
- Each parent's empathy and ability to adopt the child's position/perspective
- Each parent's own experiences of being parented
- Each parent's history of previous and current partner relationships
- Each parent's ability to understand and meet the child's physical, emotional, social and cognitive *current* as well as *changing* developmental needs
- Each parent's ability to distinguish the child's needs from his/her own
- Each parent's ability to prioritize the child's needs over his/her own needs
- Each parent's ability to manage stressful situations and impulse control
- Each parent's insight into and taking responsibility for past and current shortcomings in parenting
- Presence of and use of each parent's support/friendship network
- Each parent's approaches to disciplining and making and maintaining consistent boundaries
- Each parent's relationship with the child
- Each parent's ability to protect the child from harm (abuse and neglect)
- Each parent's ability to change, required therapeutic/other resources and timescale issues
- Each parent's ability to work in partnership with professionals and significant others
- Each parent's ability to change, make use of required therapeutic/other resources and timescale issues
- Each parent's risks to the child and self
- Psychiatric, psychological and cognitive profile of the child
- The child's past and current mental health issues/emotional trauma
- The child's current emotional, social, cognitive and behavioural functioning

- The child's attachment to each parent
- The child's attachment to/relationship with siblings
- The child's contact needs
- The most appropriate placement for the child
- The child's reasons for refusing contact
- Any therapeutic needs the child may have
- Any therapeutic needs the family may have.

In addition to the questions specified in the LOI, an agreed list of essential reading of court documents will be attached. The expert, having received the jointly agreed LOI, can request further information but this has to be agreed by all the parties first. As a result, the LOI may be modified in consultation with all the parties. This is best done in a network meeting.

Planning and starting Family Ties work

Once the initial referral or Letter of Instruction has been received, a network meeting is usually convened by the practitioner. The individuals attending a network meeting should always include both parents, any other significant members of the family network (e.g. grandparents, uncles/aunts) and involved professionals, such as a representative from the family court welfare services, for example a family court adviser and children's guardian, or a social worker. Sometimes the parents' legal representatives also want to attend as observers, though this requires the consent of all the parties. Detailed minutes of the meeting are taken and these are circulated subsequently and checked for accuracy by each person attending the network meeting. Amendments are made until there is a document which is eventually agreed by all. A network meeting assists in developing a coordinated and mutually agreed plan for the assessment and therapeutic work and it is followed up by review meetings at regular intervals of three to six weeks, involving the same constellation of professionals, parents and significant others as appropriate to the case. The aims of network meetings are summarized in Box 3.2.

Box 3.2 Aims of network meetings

1. To bring together parents, other significant carers and professionals
2. To create a map of who is involved: what each professional's input is – to whom, when and why
3. To openly hear each professional's concerns, as well as each parent's worries
4. To discuss differences of opinion openly
5. To involve parents in drawing up the assessment/therapy contract and defining what they themselves want from professionals/assessment
6. To clearly define the areas of the assessment/therapeutic work and/or refine the LOI
7. To agree on consequences of change/no change
8. To agree on who is going to carry out what work
9. To agree on a timescale for the work.

When one or both parents claim that they cannot be present in the same room together, it is in principle possible to have two network meetings in sequence: the first with one parent and the second with the other parent. In cases of extreme domestic violence and specific restraining orders this may be the only possibility of bringing the network together. However, in practice it is possible – with appropriate reassurances provided to each parent – to accommodate most parents in the same room, albeit with special arrangements in place so as to ensure the safety of each participant. In these circumstances it is particularly important for the meeting to be firmly chaired, with clear spatial and time boundaries in place.

In the light of discussions held in a network meeting the aims of the referral or questions in the Letter of Instruction can be subjected to revisions, with new questions for the clinician being formulated to provide a helpful focus.

Structuring the work

Following the network meeting, it is usually possible to draw up a plan for the proposed work. For each assessment task, the question is: 'what

Person	➔	Who?
Time	➔	When, how often, how long?
Place	➔	Where?
Activity	➔	What?

Figure 3.1 Dimensions of context for designing assessments

context needs to be created to answer that question?' and this forms the basis for the structure of the assessment and therapeutic intervention. When answering this basic question pragmatically, it is helpful to consider four types of 'context' which consist of the dimensions 'person', 'time', 'place' and 'activity' as shown in Figure 3.1 (Asen 2004). The context question needs to be answered across several levels:

The question of who should be present in a meeting or session opens up many possibilities – from children and parents to members of the wider family, to 'significant others', be they friends, religious figures or other professionals. In this way the therapeutic 'system' remains open to different people joining future sessions. When considering where to carry out the work, there are a number of options: a clinic setting, home, school, corridors of the court – the list would seem endless. Working with a child, parent or family in a naturalistic setting where the problem manifests itself can be more effective than confining all clinical work to offices or other agency-based interview rooms. The issue of when encompasses length, frequency, duration and the actual time of the session(s). Clinicians of different persuasions tend to create discrete time slots, lasting on average between 50 to 90 minutes. What actually takes place during the course of the work, the activities the child, parent or family become involved in, can also vary a great deal. This, of course, includes therapeutic conversations or discussions which tend to be word focused. However, playful activities, some of which are non- or para-verbal, such as role plays, sculpting, collages and exercises, often provide more helpful information and also present opportunities to understand interactional patterns, experimentation and change.

The contextualizing questions ('who?', 'where?', 'when?' and 'how?') need not only be asked at the initiation of work, but throughout the whole process of carrying out assessment and therapeutic work, and in collaboration with the family. By regularly involving children, parents and sometimes professionals in this questioning process it becomes possible to co-construct possible contexts for potential change.

Table 3.1 below provides one example of a work programme devised for addressing questions asked in a fairly typical Letter of Instruction. Such programmes will of course vary considerably from case to case and need to be continually reviewed in the light of information arising throughout the assessment. Even in cases where there has been prior assessment of a family and where therapeutic intervention has been recommended, it is advisable to conduct a short viability assessment with written feedback, prior to providing any form of therapeutic intervention.

Table 3.1 Work programme example

Type	Person	Place	Time	Examples of activity
Individual	Parent/carer	Clinic, home, contact centre	3 × 1 hour	Talking and listening, hypothetical scenario exploration
Individual	Child	Clinic, home, school, contact centre	3 × 40–60 mins (depending on age/engagement)	Talking and listening, activities, play, assessment tools
Individual	Liaison	Teachers, other key professionals	2–3 × 30 mins	Information gathering
Parental couple	Parents	Clinic	3 × 1 hour	Promoting collaborative working
Family	Parents/carers and children	Home, foster home, clinic, community	2–3 × 1–2 hours with each parent being assessed	Family tasks/games, talking, listening, playing, eating
Family	Parents/carers and children	Contact centre, home, clinic, community	1–2 × 1–2 hours	Observation of contact
Family	Siblings	Contact centre, home, clinic, community	2–3 × 1 hour	Family tasks/games, talking, listening, playing

Chapter 4

Assessing children

Case example

Sarah was 13 years old when she was referred to the clinic. Her parents had acrimoniously separated seven years earlier, followed by years of litigation over where she should live and how much time she should spend with each parent. She initially lived with her mother and regular contact between Sarah and her father was never firmly established. It broke down altogether after the mother made a series of allegations of physical, emotional and sexual abuse in relation to the father, which were accompanied by a range of similarly serious counter-allegations against the mother by the father. These were investigated by social care and found to be unsubstantiated on both sides. Serious allegations from both parents continued over the following months, all found to be unsubstantiated, and Sarah was eventually removed from her mother's care and placed in foster care while an independent assessment was conducted. When first assessed, Sarah presented as being outwardly warm, friendly and cheerful, disclosing a lot of personal information, but she would quickly become angry and controlling when challenged. She described her relationship with her mother in rather idealized terms, but spoke at length about her father and his alleged abusive behaviour in a demonstrative manner, seemingly aimed at eliciting the practitioner's sympathy if not outrage. When discussing the prospect of seeing her father, Sarah began to hyperventilate; she cried and asked her mother to join her in the consulting room. The mother joined and complained that her daughter was being 'forced' to be assessed and that the whole process was harmful to Sarah, whose distress continued to escalate in her mother's presence, but quickly reduced once her mother left the consulting room.

Building a relationship

It may seem grossly unfair that children – so often the victims of their parents' protracted battles – should be subjected to formal assessments. In cases where there has been extensive litigation, children have often previously been assessed by a number of professionals and they may understandably be resistant to having to talk to yet another person and having to answer almost identical questions, feeling increasingly that 'nobody is listening to me'. Thus, in order to promote engagement, it can be helpful to imagine what might be going on in the child's mind: the child may be reluctant and torn by loyalty conflicts; they may be anxious about not putting a foot wrong; they may be angry about being dragged into commenting on the inter-parental conflicts. Finding a way of acknowledging such likely thoughts and feelings helps the child feel understood: 'I can imagine that this is not easy for you, probably you didn't really feel like coming here, but maybe I am wrong ... having to come here to talk about your family ... some children whom I have seen have felt anxious, others annoyed or angry'. The practitioner can pause and leave some space for potential comments from the child or young person and then continue explaining the work context, including stating that if they cannot or do not want to answer any of the questions put to them, they can simply say, like in a quiz show: 'pass'. This can provide reassurance that this is not a cross-examination resembling a court setting: 'I don't want you to feel that you have to talk about things that you don't want to talk about ... young people often have good reasons for not wanting to do that'. The child or young person's responses to the first contacts with the practitioner can provide an early indication of their attachment representations and mentalizing capacity. It can also be informative to observe how easily children separate from their parent and the ways in which they reunite. Some children, for example, may or may not seek approval from their parent first. However, in order to draw any initial conclusions from observations, the practitioner needs to consider what might be developmentally expected and appropriate given a child or young person's age and circumstances.

The next phase of assessment involves getting to know the child and how this is done very much depends on the child's age. With children younger than five or six years old, the practitioner can invite them to look around the room and find something they want to play with. The child may focus on a toy and become preoccupied with that and the practitioner will observe how the child does this and whether or not the child involves the practitioner in the play. Observations of children's play can provide useful insights into their lives, but also information about a child's capacity to form narratives – a milestone required for the development of effective mentalizing. Therefore, it is important that the practitioner spends some time simply observing and following the child's interests and preoccupations. When, for example, the child requests: 'you be the robber and I will be the police and you do not run away', the practitioner complies with this instruction, being curious about where the child takes the play next. Some children's play can be very disjointed and incoherent. When this is consistently observed in children over four years old, this may reflect a broader problem with development or attention and emotion regulation. Once the child is engaged with the practitioner, questions can be explored through play; this may allow the reconstruction of events in a displaced fashion by, for example, using toy animals to represent different family members.

With children older than five or six, the practitioner may start by stating that 'this is the first time we've met, I know very little about you … how old you are, your school, the sort of things you like doing, what games you play, what music you like, what you like watching on TV … that sort of thing'. In other words, questions are initially not asked about the family, the parents or any conflicts in the family. Sometimes children want to talk about the issues immediately and this may have a prepared if not rehearsed quality, for example when a boy aged six stated: 'I am here because I don't want to see my father ever again, he is horrible, he has been so nasty to my mum, he always upsets all of us'. Here it is best if the practitioner also follows the lead of the child and explores what is being said as being guided by the child/young person and their preoccupations is a basic principle of all assessment work, particularly on the first occasion. This builds trust as the child can set their own agenda rather than being dominated by the practitioner's preoccupations.

When first seeing the child, it is also important to find out whether they know why they are seeing the professional. An opening question, such as 'What did your parent tell you about coming to see me/us here?', immediately contextualizes the first encounter. Younger children not infrequently answer with 'I don't know' and the practitioner may then ask whether the child can think about what sort of place this is: 'Is this a church? Is this a school? Is this a hospital? Is this a court?' After shrugging their shoulders a few times, children usually hesitate when it comes to the 'hospital' question and say 'maybe'. This allows the practitioner to follow up with 'Is someone ill?', which can open up a conversation about family problems. When children consistently claim that they do not know why they have come, the practitioner can ask the accompanying parent to join briefly and explain this to the child. This allows a first glimpse of hearing the adult narrative.

Sequence of assessment sessions

When instructed to assess families in order to advise the court and to make recommendations about residence, contact and/or therapeutic intervention, it is useful to meet with the child on three separate occasions, in weekly or fortnightly intervals. It may also be advisable to have the child brought to the clinic by a different parent or other primary carer on the first two occasions in cases where the child has contact with both parents. Ideally, the parents should do this in turn or, in cases where a child does not have contact with the distanced parent, for them to be brought by a 'neutral' person, such as a social worker, guardian or a trusted friend or relative of the distanced parent. It is obvious that children can be influenced by the parent who brings them to assessment appointments; they are usually aware that their mother or father is in the waiting area and whilst not being physically present in the consulting room, they are usually present in the child's mind. In cases where it is alleged that the child has been primed or coached by one parent, having the child brought to some of the assessment sessions by the other parent can decrease any such anxieties and suspicions.

In the second assessment session, the practitioner can pick up on themes talked about in the previous session so as to ensure narrative continuity and to further build trust with the child. Apart from initially following the child's lead and preoccupations, in the second session more direct questions can be asked, particularly in relation to the child's wishes and feelings, or specific allegations the child may have made against the distanced parent. The child's current mental state is noted and focused upon during the course of this assessment session. This encompasses the child's general appearance and behaviour, language and speech, mood, thought content and general cognitive status. How detailed this assessment is will depend on the preferences and qualifications of the practitioner. Assessment tools such as the Revised Childhood Anxiety and Depression Scale (RCADS; Chorpita et al. 2000) and the Beck Youth Inventories (BYI; Beck et al. 2001) can provide useful additional information about a child's mental state and well-being and form the basis for further conversations, as the practitioner enquires more about items positively endorsed. For example, if a child indicates that they 'worry most of the time' on the RCADS, the practitioner can ask follow-up questions about what sort of worries the child has. Such scales are most appropriate for children aged approximately seven to eight and older.

During individual meetings with the child, be those predominantly verbal or play based, the practitioner looks at the child's ability to manage their attention, to recognize and name feelings and to regulate their own emotions, as well as their ability to take different perspectives. This helps to inform the understanding of the tasks faced by the parents and helps to pitch any subsequent therapeutic interventions appropriately. At times detailed child psychiatric examinations are required if there is a suggestion that the child may suffer from a (hitherto undiagnosed) developmental disorder or a moderate or severe psychiatric condition. Asking about self-harming thoughts or actions is essential in order to inform the risk assessment. At the end of the second assessment session the practitioner will want to have collected information on a number of different domains of the child's functioning (Box 4.1)

Box 4.1 Domains of assessment of the child/young person

- 'Story'/presentation of problem behaviour
- Exploratory and problem-solving behaviours
- Ability to play and form narratives
- Interactional skills (rapport, inhibition)
- Attachment representations
- Mental state (behaviour, mood, thought, language, cognition)
- Physical state (appearance, height, weight, coordination, speech)
- Developmental state (meeting of developmental milestones)
- Strengths and resilience
- Risk to self and others.

In the third assessment session the practitioner can specifically focus on the child's wishes and feelings (see below). In addition, a few specific tasks may be set, such as 'draw your family', 'make a clay sculpture of your family' or 'here is a doll's house, set up a family and show me how they all live together'. The purpose of these tasks is to look at the representations of the family that the child has in mind, which can then be talked about in conversation with the child. Subsequent questions, such as 'And was your family always like that?' or 'What would you like that picture or sculpture to look like in a year's time?' further assist in exploring past experiences and future hopes and fears.

When families are not involved in court proceedings and the problems are less chronic, individual assessment of the child covers similar areas, but is likely to be shorter. In these cases the focus is on forming an engagement and understanding of the individual child and their experiences within the family. This can be used both in helping the parents to better understand the child and in tailoring any subsequent interventions.

The ascertainable wishes and feelings of the child

What children say may be influenced by various factors, including the number of interviews/assessments, the type of questions and the style and tone in which these are asked, as well as the practitioner's responses to the answers children are giving. The reliability and credibility of what children say is often questioned, given that they can be suggestible under certain circumstances (Ceci & Bruck 1993) and particularly if they feel vulnerable and take sides with one parent against the other. As a result, children can fail to report important events as well as reporting 'events' that, in fact, did not occur. Furthermore, they can respond erroneously to suggestive questions, particularly when these are of a forced-choice nature (Crossman et al. 2002).

Children caught between warring parents are not infrequently faced with a dreadful dilemma: whether to be honest or to be loyal when questioned (Weir 2011). Eliciting the wishes and feelings of the child in relation to contact and residence issues has to be a major assessment focus, particularly with contact-resistant children. Given that this is usually also the task of the court-appointed officer/social worker, by the time the children are seen, they will often have stated firmly more than once that they do not wish to have any form of contact with the distanced parent. Hence often the newly appointed practitioner is tasked with what appears to go against the child's expressed wishes and feelings. Obviously, the expressed wishes and feelings of children need to be ascertained and recorded. However, there is a difference between listening to and taking account of a child's wishes on the one hand, and simply acting on what the child says they want, on the other hand. Deciding what weight to give to a child's expressed wishes and feelings will depend on many factors, including the child's age and developmental stage, as well as their capacity to mentalize effectively. When child triangulation processes such as exposure to interparental conflict, the denigration of a child's relationship with the distanced parent and/or physical and emotional distance from that parent are present, the process of deciding what weight and importance to give to the child's wishes and feelings can be a very complex task. This is because the child often experiences powerful feelings such as guilt and anger as well as loyalty conflicts, leading to the development of attachment strategies aimed at protecting the care the child receives from the closer parent. Such processes can very much influence a child's beliefs and expressed wishes and feelings. Indications that a child's expressed wishes and feelings may be influenced by an attachment strategy developed in response to child triangulation processes include:

- Easily triggered, intense emotional affect and demonstrative non-verbal behaviours of the child in relation to the prospect of contact which elicit immediate caregiving responses/approval from the closer parent
- Inability/unwillingness to discuss rationally and calmly any positive aspects of the distanced parent or their past relationship with the child
- Trivial reasons given for demonizing the distanced parent
- Wishes and feelings cannot be questioned without outbursts of emotion or strong challenges from the child.

Signs and dynamics seen in children which suggest some form of child triangulation and alienating processes are listed in Box 4.2 (after Gardner 1998; Kelly & Johnston 2001; Gorell Barnes 2017; Chimera 2018). In our experience, these signs can also be seen in families where children have developed strong loyalty bonds with one parent as a result of exposure to inter-parental conflict or when there has been lengthy emotional and/or physical separation from a parent with whom the child had a previously good relationship.

Box 4.2 Common signs and dynamics in children that suggest the presence of triangulation processes

- Denigration and rejection of a previously loved parent
- Only speaks negatively about and 'bad-mouths' the rejected parent
- Has a narrative about the rejected parent that has a rehearsed quality
- Provides minor, weak, frivolous or even absurd reasons for denigrating the rejected parent
- Displays no feelings of remorse, shame or guilt when denigrating the rejected parent, with coldness and absence of empathy
- Has polarized views of the parents, with the closer parent being 'good' and the rejected parent being 'bad', with a lack of ambivalence
- Always fully agrees with the closer parent's views and position, takes sides with and defends the favoured parent under every circumstance, like an 'automatic reflex'
- Uses similar, or even 'borrowed', phrases and language as the closer parent
- Insists he/she has come to the decision independently and that their negative views of the rejected parent are not influenced by the closer parent or anyone else
- Is dismissive about the rejected parent's family and friends
- Has age-inappropriate knowledge of the court case, financial arrangements and other adult matters
- Has economic narratives which are thrown in the rejected parent's face ('you didn't give us any money to live on')
- Is very rude to the rejected parent and has very emotional outbursts ('I can't call you daddy anymore because you are not really my daddy anymore; why did you do this to us? You have spoilt our lives. I hate you to death')
- Texts threatening messages and images and/or makes physical threats to the rejected parent
- Claims that the rejected parent's contact requests are responsible for poor school performance/physical and psychological symptoms and illness.

Merely focusing on what children actually say in response to questions about their wishes and feelings can be a rather unreliable indicator as children in these scenarios often have such conflicted feelings. Furthermore, the official weight given by the court to establishing children's expressed wishes and feelings may encourage parental manipulation. Yet, children want to feel heard and be listened to and have the opportunity to express their loyalty to the closer parent. The practitioner's default position has to be to carefully listen to children's expressed wishes and feelings, however rehearsed their narrative may appear at first. When exploring what the child wants in relation to contact, the ensuing conversation needs to be extended beyond mere 'yes' or 'no' responses. Various techniques can help here. For example, the practitioner can introduce playful and creative techniques, such as jointly making a comic strip about what happened during the last contact and then designing together a new comic strip about how the child would have liked things to have turned out. With younger children a toy phone can be used to pretend to call different family members in a playful manner to make arrangements for talking to or meeting the rejected parent. Listening to the child's account does not mean that it has to be accepted: the child's best interests, as assessed by the professionals and the court, may have to override what the child him/herself may believe is in their best interest.

It is also important to ascertain the child's wishes and feelings beyond the immediate issue of contact, namely about their relationship with the distanced parent in the future. Individual work with the child should establish what they feel they need from the distanced parent in order to move forward. This can include an apology for past hurtful behaviours and parental acknowledgement of some responsibility for what has gone wrong. It can also include reasonable requests for change in the distanced parent, such as paying the child more attention, being more affectionate, avoiding shouting, or not sharing information about the legal proceedings with them.

Assessing attachment

When in the court arena, most jointly agreed Letters of Instruction request the specific assessment of the child's attachment to each caregiver. There are a number of formal attachment assessments which have been designed for scientific and research purposes, but it is not unproblematic to use these in clinical practice (Byrne et al. 2005). While the assessment procedures require specific training and their evaluation tends to be time consuming and costly, some components of the assessment tools can be employed by practitioners and can give an excellent description of internalized attachment representations. It is obvious that in cases where one of the parents has not had contact with their child for a long time – years rather than months – there is little to be gained from formally assessing the child's attachment to the distanced parent. This is likely not to be a helpful measure as it is possible that due to the long absence of that parent from the child's life and because of triangulation processes the child's attachment representation will be skewed – and therefore any 'finding' will have little predictive value as to the child's ability to form a secure attachment with that parent in the future. Finally, while structured assessments can provide an indication of a child's attachment patterns, they should not be used in isolation. Information gained from such procedures needs to be considered alongside observations in different contexts and from different sources; it also needs to be viewed within the context of the cultural and social identity of the family, including its specific culture-mediated caregiving roles. Furthermore, practitioners need to widen their perspective beyond the mere interactions between the child and parent(s) and also focus on the wider caregiving system around the child and consider how this affects the identity formation of the child.

The strange situation assessment

An adaptation of this assessment procedure, first pioneered by Ainsworth and Bell (1970), can be employed to assess attachment styles of children under the age of three years. It is carried out with each parent in turn and usually on different days. The parent is asked to suddenly leave the consulting room, telling the child that they will be 'back soon'. This procedure provides an opportunity for observing the child's reactions and behaviours on separation and reunification. A child who is securely attached to a caregiver will usually happily explore a room and toys, using their parent as a 'secure base' to return to and reference. When the parent suddenly leaves for a brief period, the child will usually show some distress, but be fairly easily soothed upon the parent's return. Insecurely attached children will usually be fairly inhibited in their exploration, preferring to stay close to the parent, or explore widely, making little reference to the parent. When the parent leaves they may become quickly distressed and take a very long time to calm upon return, or appear largely indifferent to the parent's comings and goings. Children with disorganized attachment styles tend to demonstrate no consistent and coherent pattern in relation to a new situation and the parent's comings and goings.

Observations of the separation and reunion behaviours can provide useful information about children of any age when they follow the practitioner to the consulting room and leave their parents in the waiting room. However, any interactions must be interpreted with caution since this form of separation is not unexpected as it is in the classic strange situation procedure. Nevertheless, excessively clingy behaviours or aloofness on separation may indicate attachment difficulties. As children get older, disorganized attachment styles can manifest as excessively controlling behaviour. However, as with all components of the assessment of children, conclusions cannot be drawn on the basis of one single observation. A child's attachment behaviour can only be adequately understood when observed on several occasions in different contexts. Some children are excessively clingy towards one parent in the assessment context, but appear to have no problems separating in other contexts – thus the attachment behaviour may be specific to the parents' conflict around contact.

Story stems

The Story Stem Assessment Profile (SSAP; Hodges et al. 2003) is an assessment tool that can be used with children between the ages of four and nine years and is designed to elicit information about their representations of their parent(s) and caregiving. Children are presented with the beginnings of a sequence of stories, both spoken and played out with doll and animal figures, in a dramatic way so as to activate the attachment system. They are then invited to complete the story in their own way and are asked by the practitioner to 'show me and tell me what happens next'. Children's perceptions and expectations of family roles and relationships, as well as their attachment representations, can be assessed without asking them direct or potentially intrusive questions about their parents which might generate anxieties or loyalty conflicts. In addition, information can be gained about children's internal working models by watching how they play and narrate games that involve caregiving behaviours, such as play with baby dolls, doctors and police and emergency vehicles. The practitioner can increase arousal by creating pretend emergency situations that bring forth responses more likely to be connected with the child's attachment representations.

The Child Attachment Interview

In its pure form the Child Attachment Interview (CAI) is a semi-structured interview for children aged seven to 12 (Target et al. 2003; Shmueli-Goetz et al. 2004). It is based on the Adult Attachment Interview (AAI), adapted for children by focusing on representations of relationships with parents and attachment-related events. Unlike the AAI, the CAI focuses upon current memories (rather than retrospective accounts) and assesses children's perceptions of their attachment figures' current availability and sensitive responsiveness through eliciting internal representations of the main attachment figures. Areas of interest are examples of preoccupied anger, anxious depressive ruminative preoccupation, idealization of attachment figures, dismissal of attachment and the resolution of conflicts. Building a profile of a child's attachment in this way can be very informative, but it is also time consuming. Practitioners use and adapt some of the components of the CAI by asking the child questions that are likely to connect with attachment representations, for example, to describe the following: what it is like to be with the parent in a few words; what happens when the parent gets cross; how the child felt when that happened; what the child thinks the parent felt when he/she told him off; to speak about a time when the child was upset and wanted help or when the child was ill or got hurt; what the child felt when the parents argued. As with all the formal measures of attachment described here, the responses cannot be formally coded unless administered and scored by a practitioner who has completed the appropriate training.

Creating a relationship map

To assist the practitioner's understanding of the child's perception of their relationships with both parents and members of their respective families of origin, a relationship map can be constructed with the child on a large piece of paper. This map can also include significant others, such as friends and professionals. There are various ways in which one can construct 'eco-maps' of the child's life (see for example

Bing 1970; Burns & Harvard Kaufman 1970; Geddes & Medway 1977). These recognize that seeing relationships drawn may be more meaningful to children, as maps provide a graphic and visual account of their relationship network. The practitioner can introduce the family relationship map to the child by stating: 'I would like to find out a bit more about you and your family and also your friends and other people who help you. Let us draw together who is important to you and let us say that this circle here in the middle is you. Now here is the pen, I would like you to draw other circles to show all the other people important to you – family members, friends, people who help you. You can put the people who are really important close to you and those who are less important a bit further away. Also draw them like circles, big or small and put a name or a letter next to them so that you remember who is who. Spend a few minutes doing this now and then we can talk about it.'

Sometimes children want to explain who is who as they draw, sometimes they want to finish the map before they want to explain what they have done: 'Would you like to tell me who is who?' and once the child has begun to talk, the practitioner can ask for clarification: 'And how do you get on with him/her?' and 'What do you really like about that person? And is there anything you don't like about him/her?'

Eco-maps of this kind can be used as a tool for discussing relationships. When there are siblings, it may help to understand aspects of the child's relationship with them. Furthermore, questions can be asked about the relationship of the siblings with each parent: 'Who likes your dad most? Who loves your mum the most? Who finds it most difficult to talk with her? Why might that be? When you quarrel with your sister/brother, what happens next? Does mum/dad take sides? Why might that be?'

Assessing children's allegations of abuse by the distanced parent

It is not uncommon in entrenched contact and residence cases for children to make spurious and often unsubstantiated claims of past abuse by the distanced parent. These usually relate to events in the past, when the child's parents still lived together, and have only emerged a long time after the parents' separation. Whilst there is frequently some or a lot of truth in the allegations made, the account can be very exaggerated or dramatized. Box 4.3 (adapted after Weir

2011) lists the main factors requiring consideration when trying to establish whether or not the allegations of abuse by the distanced parent are truthful, false or exaggerated.

Box 4.3 Likelihood of false allegations of abuse

- Allegations have a robotic and rehearsed quality (need to differentiate from disassociation)
- Statements are inconsistent – both internally and across statements
- Evidence of developmentally unusual sexual knowledge/ language
- Use of adult words and concepts
- Child's eagerness to talk about the abuse, without appropriate or congruent affect (e.g. painful, depressed, anxious)
- Lack of convincing details and difficulty elaborating or providing examples
- Overstating/exaggerating case
- Report of allegation(s) originates initially from the closer parent
- Closer parent refuses to allow the child to be seen without her/him being present
- Closer parent appears to be 'pleased' about the disclosure
- Disclosure elicits exaggerated caregiving responses and attention from the closer parent
- Closer parent repeatedly prompts or reminds the child about the allegations
- Closer parent encourages the child to repeat the allegations to everyone
- Allegations have a level of detail incongruent with the age of the child at the time the abuse is reported to have taken place (e.g. the child recalling in detail events that happened when they were a toddler)
- Closer parent continues to engage a number of experts until the alleged abuse is substantiated
- Child is very comfortable in the presence of the allegedly abusive parent.

Assessing the presence of emotional abuse and neglect

Emotional abuse and neglect is present when there are persistent harmful parent–child interactions, characterized by acts of both omission and commission, which can have severe and persistent adverse effects on the child's emotional development. Emotional abuse/neglect is not a one-off event or isolated incident but a process. Gabarino (1978) described five types of emotionally abusive behaviours: rejecting, isolating, terrorizing, ignoring and corrupting. The five categories of emotional abuse described by Glaser (2002), can be helpfully considered when assessing children who are embroiled in child triangulation processes:

1. Emotional unavailability, unresponsiveness and neglect of the child are present when parents become over-preoccupied with the ongoing inter-parental conflicts and/or are consequently anxious or distressed, resulting in being frequently emotionally unavailable to their children.

2. Negative attributions to the child leading to rejection and harsh punishment can develop when the distanced parent is denigrated and when the child is said to have 'inherited' specific negative personality traits from the demonized parent ('you are just like your father'). Here the child's character is portrayed as 'bad' or flawed and in addition to feeling worthless, unloved and rejected, the child may also be punished for seemingly acting like the distanced parent, for defending them or wanting to spend time with them.

3. Unrealistic expectations, overprotection, inappropriate ways of disciplining, exposure to disturbing or frightening experiences (e.g. domestic violence) are all manifestations of developmentally inappropriate and inconsistent parental interactions with the child. Parents can place excessive and unreasonable demands on a child or expose their child to drastic mood changes or sudden emotional outbursts. This can include being used as a confidante by the closer parent and becoming exposed to inappropriate adult information.

4. The failure to recognize the child's individuality and psychological boundaries, and using the child for the fulfilment of the adult's needs can manifest itself when parents infantilize their child in order to meet their own need to be 'needed', or when

a parent attributes their own feelings of fear or anger to their child, or when the child is used as a 'pawn' in disputes with the ex-partner.

5. Finally, the failure to promote the child's social adaptation is present, for example, when parents disrupt the child's need to be part of and adapt to their social environment. This can happen when a child loses contact with key members of the distanced parent's extended family and friendship network. Isolating children or exposing them to antisocial values also comes under this category of emotional abuse and neglect, as does the exposure to unsafe or troubled environments.

Practitioners may first suspect some form of emotional abuse/neglect when a child seeks parental approval to the extreme and is most anxious to conform to instructions. The possibility of emotional abuse/neglect may also be considered when a child is very passive and clingy, or when the child behaves in very age-inappropriate – either 'adultified' or very infantile – manner, or when the child presents as being very withdrawn and apathetic.

Assessing capacity and consent

When assessing children who refuse to have contact with a distanced or rejected parent, the question often arises as to whether this may be due to the excessive influence of the favoured parent and if so, whether the child has the capacity to make his/her own decisions. Children can be, or may feel, pressured into refusing contact by one of their parents and this is particularly the case when the child is emotionally very dependent on one parent, thus making them less likely to resist the influence. The stronger the emotionally dependent relationship, the greater the ability of the 'persuader' (the parent) to influence or override the decision-making process of the child or young person.

When considering the issue of 'legal competence', practitioners are guided by a test of competency. In England, Gillick competency (or the Gillick standard) identifies the capacity of children under the age of 16 to consent to their own assessment and treatment. The term 'legal competence' implies that a child or young person demonstrates sufficient understanding and intelligence to fully understand what is being proposed and to give instructions to a solicitor, thereby having the capacity to make decisions for themselves. Competence to give consent comes incrementally with growing maturity and experience. Furthermore, a child may be competent to make autonomous decisions in some areas but not in others, as children's abilities develop gradually over time and at different rates.

In the context of court proceedings, the question of whether or not children have sufficient intellectual and emotional maturity to make fully informed decisions relates primarily to the matter of contact and where they wish to live. The questions to be answered would therefore usually be as follows:

- Does the child fully understand the need for a change of residence?
- Does the child fully understand the need for contact with the distanced parent?
- Does the child fully understand what any changes of current arrangements involve and what the changes are for?
- Does the child understand the probable long-term and short-term benefits and risks and what the alternatives are?
- Does the child have the ability to consider the wider implications of their decision, including moral and family questions?

In answering these questions, the practitioner has to first consider the child's factual understanding of the issues and the alternatives, as these are necessary for any person giving informed consent, and whether this understanding is comprehensive. The child's rational decision-making processes also require assessment and whether these are influenced by fears of having an opinion that is different from the parent's. Finally, the practitioner has to assess the child's appreciation of the personal implications of specific decisions, including any possible short- and long-term effects on their own development and their relationships with family and friends.

Collecting additional information on the child

Practitioners also need to obtain independent information from other sources in order to build a comprehensive picture of the child. This includes information about various domains, including

- Academic performance
- Peer relations
- Behaviour, attention and concentration

- How and whether the child seeks adult help
- Their attitude to learning, separation and reunion
- Self-care and organizational skills
- The school's relationship with each parent
- How the child presents before and after attending the assessment and contacts with the distanced parent.

The accounts of members of the extended family, friends, social worker(s) or other professionals complete the picture. Medical records are sometimes needed, particularly when fabricated or induced illness (FII) is suspected.

Parental misuse of diagnoses

When, after a thorough assessment, a formal child psychiatric diagnosis is made, the parents may blame each other for making their child 'ill'. Parental concerns about the implications of a specific diagnosis may be so intense that children themselves can become affected, further compounding their own already existing anxieties. Parents can also claim that 'making' the child have contact with the distanced parent induces acute panic states and also leads to unsettled and/or disruptive behaviours following contact, and the parent may seek professional validation of such concerns by, for example, getting the GP to confirm these. Instead of getting drawn into a potentially blaming search for which parent caused emotional harm to the child, practitioners achieve more when they focus on what each parent can specifically do to improve the child's mental health.

Chapter 5

Assessing parents

'Good enough' parenting

Each child has physical, emotional, social, cognitive and spiritual needs and parenting assessments focus on how and whether parents are able to meet these. Many of these needs are universal and basic, such as the need for food and shelter, or the need for physical and emotional safety and security. Other needs are very specific to each individual child's physical and psychological make-up. Yet further needs are environmentally and culturally determined and embedded. As almost all children are born into and grow up in families, for them to thrive requires a 'good enough' fit between their needs and the capacity of their parents or other primary caregivers to meet these needs. However, there is considerable controversy as to what may constitute 'good enough' parenting and only very few people believe in the concept of a 'perfect parent'. 'Good enough' parents may be expected to have a whole range of distinct characteristics, including being loving and empathic, listening to their children's worries and aspirations, nurturing their self-esteem and confidence, being both flexible and limit setting, providing guidance, supporting the child's relationship with the other parent and important members of both extended families – and more.

When assessing parents in the context of legal proceedings in relation to residence and contact issues, the focus should be on their strengths and shortcomings as a *parent* and how these affect the child–parent relationship (Budd 2001), as well as identifying protective and risk factors to the child (Asen 2006; Gould & Martindale 2007). In the relevant literature it is reported that specific psychopathology and personality disorders are present in a significant proportion of high-conflict parents litigating over contact and residence issues (see, for example, Johnston 1993; Feinberg & Greene 1997; Barwick et al. 2003; Friedman 2004). It is also suggested that these parents may therefore be more likely to be rigidly defensive and moralistic, that they perceive themselves to be flawless and virtuous, externalizing responsibility onto others and lacking insight into their own behaviours and their impact on others (Siegel 1996; Bathurst et al. 1997; Bagby et al. 1999). Some practitioners have detected an increased prevalence of personality disorders among severely alienating parents (Neff & Cooper 2004; Baker 2007). Other studies, for example Stewart (2001) and Brown (2008), found that parents frequently presented with domestic violence, substance misuse and criminal behaviour. Relationship characteristics of these parents included mistrust, poor sense of boundaries, tendencies to draw children into the inter-parental disputes, involvement of child welfare agencies in the disputes, allegations of sexual abuse and frequent changes of legal representatives. Such findings can help to inform practitioners before they begin an assessment and also assist when identifying some potential risk factors. However, practitioners need to be careful not to make assumptions about levels of psychopathology in any parent prior to actually meeting and assessing them so that in each case the strengths and weaknesses of each parent are carefully assessed and the impact on their parenting capacity is properly determined. It is important to stress, throughout the assessment, that the aim of the work is for the child(ren) to have appropriate relationships with *both* parents and for them to no longer be affected by inter-parental conflicts.

In the Family Ties approach, when conducting assessments for the court, each parent is seen on their own on three separate occasions, in assessment sessions which last 60 to 90 minutes and usually take place over a period of four weeks. The main areas relevant for assessing high-conflict parents are as follows:

- Problem history
- History of being parented and 'lessons' learned
- History of parenting their own child(ren)
- Ability to mentalize the child(ren)
- Capacity for self-reflection
- Parenting competencies
- Emotional and behavioural self-regulation
- Presence of child triangulation processes
- Portrayal of the other parent
- Current and past parental mental health issues
- Forensic history and information on substance/alcohol misuse.

Case example

The parents of Adam, aged eight, and Ryan, aged ten, divorced three years prior to attending the clinic. Both children subsequently refused to have any form of contact with their father. Court proceedings were instigated by the father, with both parents claiming that the other parent was suffering from serious mental health issues. The mother, Ms I, claimed that the children's father, Mr J, was a 'psychopath'; that he had been cruel, abusive and highly controlling towards her and the children; and that he was very good at manipulating professionals. Mr J referred to his ex-wife as a 'very damaged woman', adding that she had experienced sexual abuse as a child and that, as a result, she had developed a personality disorder, was abusing drugs and would on occasion self-harm by hitting herself. As to his own life, Mr J said that he had experienced stress and depression associated with difficult life events, but never received or needed any psychological treatment. Ms I spoke about having been sexually abused as a child by a family friend, and how she had 'gone off the rails' as a teenager. She said that she had never been diagnosed with any mental health problem or received psychological treatment. She acknowledged that there had been times in the past when she was emotionally unavailable to the children due to her own distress. Formal personality inventory assessments indicated that both parents presented with a 'turbulent' personality type, but with no other disorder. However, the results also indicated that both parents had attempted to respond in a socially desirable manner and disclosed little.

Listening to parental narratives

When first meeting it is important that each parent feels that the practitioner has listened to their story of 'how it all happened'. This requires time and patience as it is not unlikely that the parental narrative will be dominated by how 'mad' or 'bad' the other parent is and how much of a 'victim' the reporting parent is and/or has been. The practitioner may state that the whole time of the first assessment session will be reserved for the parent's account – 'the story so far' – but that all the subsequent sessions will focus on 'how things are now and how they can be different in the future'. Difficult though this may be at times, the practitioner has to be respectful of each parent's problem definition, including who the parent believes 'has the problem'. The practitioner's stance is supportive, empathically validating each parent's emotional experience and not challenging the narrative at this stage, attempting to see the situation through each parent's 'eyes', as it were.

There is often an understandable tendency on each parent's part to try and get the practitioner to understand only their perspective, losing sight of their child's needs in the process. The positioning of the practitioner is therefore crucial, since if either parent feels that the practitioner is 'on the side' of the other, the risks of either disengaging from the assessment process or attempting to involve the practitioner directly in the ongoing conflict are high. This may require the practitioner to adopt an understanding and supportive stance whilst exploring each parent's narrative ('I think I can see why this is, or was, upsetting you') and remaining explicitly neutral in relation to the other (absent) parent (Rait 2000). In order for the practitioner to maintain an alliance with the parent and yet not become involved in seemingly taking sides with one parent against the other, it is useful to validate the parent's struggle and distress rather than their actual beliefs or views. This also models a mentalizing stance as it involves the possibility of holding two different perspectives simultaneously. For example, if a parent has been found by the court to have made unsubstantiated allegations that the ex-partner sexually abused their child, but is unable to accept the Finding of Fact made by the court, the practitioner can empathize with the parent's experience of being concerned for their child's welfare and believing something to be true and not being believed, while simultaneously having to endorse a different 'truth', as pronounced by the court. Parents also feel understood and empathized with when they are given credit for the role they may have played in any positive developments their child has achieved – another important 'joining' move (Gottlieb 2012).

When parents are literally 'married' to their 'story' which they and those close to them fully embrace or even 'live', appropriate respect is required. This may initially encourage the parent to produce further problem-saturated narratives, i.e. long and circumstantial accounts of what happened or explanations which sound well practised and have in all likelihood been recited before when talking to other professionals. The stance of pausing and repeating what the individual parent has said allows the practitioner to remain connected and alert and not be tempted to simply switch off. Disrupting a well-worn narrative by slowing it down and asking questions, including questions about how other people might have viewed what went on, can be an effective way to bring in potentially different perspectives. It is a fairly common phenomenon that at the end of the first assessment session the practitioner will be (almost) convinced by a specific parent's narrative, possibly building up an unfavourable picture of the other (absent) parent. This, however, usually gets quickly undone when subsequently listening to the other parent's narrative. During both initial assessment sessions the practitioner takes note of how much of each parent's account is actually focused on the child(ren) and their predicament – and how much each parent is preoccupied with their own hardship and suffering, and with blaming and criticizing the other parent.

The history of being parented – 'lessons' learned or not?

The exploration of how each parent's own experiences of being parented are impacting on their ability to parent their child(ren) can be undertaken during the course of the first assessment session if time permits or, alternatively, at the beginning of the second assessment session, with open questions about each parent's childhood and, a bit later, with more specific questions: 'Tell me about what sort of mother your mother was – and what sort of father your father was. What did your mother do really well? What not so well? What did you decide to do yourself when you became a mother? What did you want to do differently as a mother?'

Parents' own attachment experiences will affect their capacity for emotional self-regulation and can thus impact on their interactions with partners and children. Many families have repetitive communication and interaction patterns, which occur so regularly and predictably that they seem 'scripted' (Byng-Hall 1986). Embedded family stories are handed down from one generation to the next and can affect their beliefs and actions. However, family scripts are not written in stone: they can be replicated, corrected or altogether dismissed (Byng-Hall 1995). Which of these options families and their individual members pursue will depend on many different factors, including attachment relationships within the family of origin and the relationships the parent has gone on to make in adult life. For example, violent family experiences may generate particular sensitivities, and individuals exposed to inter-parental hostility and acrimony in childhood may, when they themselves are adults, consciously avoid becoming involved in relationships that resemble those of their parents, attempting to correct an all-too-familiar family script (Asen & Fonagy 2017a). Yet, the attraction of the familiar may be tempting and lead a parent to expose themselves and their children to scenarios that are all too similar to those they and *their* parents found themselves in, and to show mastery by generating a different outcome. Other individuals may feel, possibly without realizing, that they must not be disloyal by doing better than their own parents did.

The ability to mentalize the child

Obtaining a description from a parent of their child allows the practitioner to get the parent's picture of the child – or at least the picture that the parent wishes to paint of their child. The phrase 'tell me about your child, his/her strengths and also his/her weaknesses, if any' constitutes an invitation to do so. When one parent has been distanced from a child for some time, it is not infrequent that each parent provides quite different descriptions of their child's state of mind. Significant disparities can be explored further and it is an important part of the assessment to ask parents to reconstruct in detail a specific episode or event when the child was likely to have been affected by interparental conflict. The parents' ability to disentangle the feeling states and intentions of all those involved at the time and how these states of mind may have been connected, including the impact on their child, can provide helpful information with regard to their ability to mentalize their child. Another valuable source of information is the assessment of the parents' mentalizing capacity during 'live' interactions with their child (see Chapter 6).

A parent's mentalizing capacity can be formally assessed via the Parent Development Interview (PDI; Slade et al. 2003; Slade 2005). This is a 45-item semi-structured clinical interview intended to examine parents' current representations of their children, themselves as parents, and their relationships with their children. Interview questions can be adapted and used during parent assessment, including the following: describing what they like and dislike about the child; describing their relationship with the child and talking about a time when they and their child 'clicked'; outlining what gives them the most joy and pain as a parent; remembering a time recently when they had been angry as a parent; explaining how being a parent has changed them and how they may – or may not – want to be a parent just like their own parent(s). These and other questions help to evaluate each parent's understanding of their own and their child's internal experiences at times of heightened affective arousal – however, appropriate training is required to formally administer and code the PDI.

Capacity for self-reflection

The ability to look at oneself from the outside and to consider one's own mental states is a very important part of effective mentalizing. It is a form of self-awareness – an awareness of one's internal feelings, like emotional pain and anger, of the internal conflicts and contradictions we carry within ourselves, of doubts and vulnerabilities, and an awareness of one's limitations and weaknesses. These internal mental states are sometimes difficult to tune into and sometimes people find it easier to look at themselves through the eyes of others. After all, the sense of self is, at least in part, constructed by the ways we believe others see us. The capacity for self-reflection can be assessed by getting parents to imagine how others see them, including through the eyes of their best friend, a parent or grandparent, the allocated social worker or the child's guardian, a judge, psychiatrist and so on. Looking at themselves through the eyes of their own children and at different times of the life span – retrospectively (early childhood), now and prospectively (e.g. in ten years' time) – can also assist parents to adopt a self-reflective mode.

The ability to be self-reflective is important to enable parents to differentiate their own internal states from those of their children. Novick and Novick (2005) describe parents who seem to be blind to the separate needs and experiences of their child and instead relate to their child as if they are an externalized part of themselves. This can result in the child becoming unable to see themselves as separate from their parent: the child can experience an apparent 'self' reflected back that actually belongs to the parent, rather than to the child – an 'alien self' (Fonagy et al. 2002). This parent–child dynamic can become particularly problematic as the child grows older and is not allowed to have his/her own views or differences of opinion when, for example, valuing the distanced parent and expressing the wish to have a relationship with that parent.

Assessing parenting competencies

The comprehensive assessment of parenting capacity is a broad and complex task and a detailed description is beyond the scope of this book. Parenting competencies are diverse and include disciplinary style, attunement and empathy, providing safety, being emotionally available, encouraging curiosity and safe exploration of the outside world, supporting children's interests and individuality – and so on.

Parenting tasks vary and change and depend on the specific needs of the child, including the age and developmental stage of the child and their unique characteristics, as well as on cultural norms and related expectations of parenting.

When cases are in court, specific areas of concern about parenting capacity have usually already been raised, and assessments or investigations exist and are provided to the practitioner as part of the legal bundle (Asen 2000). Even when the court has not yet been involved, parents may already be very focused on what they regard as the other parent's inadequacies. Indeed, limited or inadequate parenting skills – rather than actual abuse – on the part of the distanced parent need to be considered as a possible reason for the child rejecting contact with the parent, or being more vulnerable to being negatively influenced by the closer parent. While it is important to investigate areas of existing concern and risk, it is also important not to focus on these areas to the exclusion of other areas of parenting. A broad and comprehensive overview of each parent's strengths and weaknesses can both inform recommendations with regard to contact and residence issues and also, where appropriate, therapeutic intervention. High-conflict parents are often very focused on the other parent's presumed or real deficits. Ascertaining their ability to reflect on any shortcomings *they themselves* may have as a parent is another important aspect of assessment and can be elicited by questions like: 'Is there anything that *you* as a parent feel you could do better – if so, can you explain this?' This encourages self-reflection and parents may find it helpful to imagine how their best friend, their mother or father, a social worker or judge might view their parenting and any potential shortcomings. As a further step, a parent can be asked to consider the following: 'Imagine that you are your three-year-old daughter looking at you, what might she say is the one thing she'd worry about most?' or 'Put yourself in the head of your son … pretend you are him … imagine what he feels when he sees you being worried about him seeing his father? What do you think goes on in his head? And might there be something he would feel too embarrassed to tell you about how he feels about his father?' Whether or not parents are able to see themselves as a parent through their child's eyes provides valuable information, not just about their capacity to parent, but also their ability to be flexible and to adopt different perspectives.

Emotional and behavioural self-regulation

One major assessment area concerns parents' emotional competencies. The range of parental emotions and ability to manage these emotions particularly when stressed, the presence or absence of parental warmth and affection, contextual fluctuations of affect – all need to be explored during the course of a parenting assessment. This can be done by obtaining detailed descriptions from the parent of situations or incidents when affection was absent or when anger and frustration prevailed and when they may have temporarily 'lost it'. The parent's account may omit or minimize specific incidents and the practitioner will therefore have to consult the court bundle to ascertain whether this contains contradictory information and discuss any disparities with the parent.

Loss of the ability to manage one's feelings is linked to the capacity to mentalize, and difficulties in mentalizing are most commonly indicators of some form of stress. Whatever the nature of the pressure on individuals, most people at times lose their capacity to think about the thoughts and feelings of others – be that children or ex-partners – when functioning in fight–flight mode (Luyten et al. 2009). A parent or child's difficulty with mentalizing can be linked specifically to the relationship context, to a memory of trauma when triggered, to general stress and fatigue, and/or to an early experience of insecure attachment and developmental trauma. For example, quite dramatic temporary failures of mentalizing can arise during emotionally intense interchanges which trigger high arousal and these literally 'turn off' the prefrontal cortex which normally mediates this specific psychological capacity: the ability to check and evaluate one's own mental states then becomes drastically limited, causing grossly inaccurate or even malevolent feelings and intentions to be attributed to others. As a result, feelings of resentment and mistrust can develop in the context of the relationship. This, in turn, increases arousal and sets in motion a negative cycle of mentalizing failure (Asen & Fonagy 2012b). When, for example, during a major argument with the mother of his daughter a father becomes convinced that the daughter is unfairly siding with the mother, he may temporarily only view his child as 'provocative' and 'unfair' and become incapable of seeing her in any other way. His accusations can trigger his daughter to behave according to this description. It is important in each case to establish a 'mentalizing profile' of the parents, and develop an understanding of the extent of their capacity to mentalize, and what might impair this capacity.

Assessing the presence of child triangulation processes

Similar to specific signs and dynamics seen in children (see Chapter 4), there are also signs observable in both the closer and distanced parents, as listed in Box 5.1 (adapted from Kelly & Johnston 2001; Gorell Barnes 2017; Chimera 2018) that can indicate the presence of child triangulation processes.

Box 5.1 Common signs and dynamics of potentially triangulating processes

The closer parent

- Believes the child does not need the other parent in their life
- Believes the distanced parent poses a risk to the child
- States that the distanced parent never loved or cared for the child
- Limits/interferes with parenting time (e.g. arranges other activities during scheduled contact time and/or gives the child 'choice' as to whether to have contact or not)
- Limits/interferes with indirect contact (e.g. social media, phone, email, etc.)
- Limits/interferes with symbolic contact (never a mention of and no photographs of the distanced parent, changing the child's surname without consent, referring to the distanced parent by derogatory names)
- Limits/interferes with the provision of information (e.g. withholding medical/educational information, using the child as a messenger, cutting off all communication between the child and the other parent)
- Demonizes the other parent systematically, to the child, the child's friends and extended family members
- Threatens the child directly/indirectly with withdrawal of love/privileges if the child enjoys contact with the other parent and/or speaks positively about that parent
- Turns the child into a confidante and/or secret keeper.

The distanced parent

- Withdraws in the face of conflict and assumes a passive stance
- Is offended by the child's lack of respect and ingratitude
- Has rigid and harsh parenting styles
- Can be self-centred
- Finds it difficult to differentiate the child's rejecting behaviours from the motivations and actions of the closer parent
- Minimizes or denies any contribution they may have made towards the child's rejection of them
- Exposes the child to their feelings of anger and/or hostility towards the other parent
- Actively encourages the child to 'stop lying' and discredits the other parent.

The portrayal of the other parent

How each parent describes the positive characteristics and strengths of their ex-partner as a *parent* can provide important information about their ability to promote a positive image of the distanced parent to their children. Parents involved in chronic litigation find the task of identifying anything positive about the other parent very much harder than talking endlessly about that parent's real or alleged shortcomings which, generally, often do not relate to their parenting skills but to their role as the ex-partner. When pressed further, closer parents typically claim that they 'never ever say anything bad' about the rejected parent. When asked whether their child is aware of the closer parent's negative views of the other parent, the most frequent answer is 'no ... we don't talk about him/her'. The practitioner may then ask the parent what he/she imagines their child feels about the fact that the distanced parent is never talked about or that nothing positive is ever said about the rejected parent's positive characteristics. A task can then be given to the closer parent to return to the next assessment session with a list, containing no fewer than five items, of the other parent's positive characteristics as a parent.

The distanced parent can also be accused of taking drugs or alcohol and this may be used as a reason for refusing contact with the child. Such accusations can be based on fact or they may be malicious – and practitioners and other professionals need to follow them up, corroborating or disproving them. It is generally thought that substance misuse – be that the regular use of illicit drugs or alcohol – eventually leads to inadequate parenting. Substance misuse can fuel acrimonious interactions and lead to major incidents of domestic violence and repeated loss of self-control. Furthermore, parental responsiveness to their children's needs can be markedly reduced and/or be inconsistent when a parent is under the influence of alcohol or other drugs. When the closer parent is misusing substances, there is the risk that dependent children may move into a quasi-parental role, acting like young carers. The chronicity and frequency of substance misuse needs to be assessed, though in practice it is often not easy to get parents to be truthful about the full extent of their consumption. Hair strand tests at regular intervals can ensure that a parent's claims of being drug-free can be corroborated.

Assessing parental mental health

In the course of entrenched parental dispute it is not uncommon for one parent to claim that the other parent is 'mad', possibly because they sincerely believe this to be the case or, at times, as a manoeuvre to disqualify him/her from being a parent. As a result, one or both parents will seek to confirm their claims by commissioning lengthy psychological and/or psychiatric reports. The terms 'mad' or 'mentally ill' are often employed in rather indiscriminate ways and do not necessarily imply that the person is actually suffering from some form of mental illness or disorder, or that it affects their parenting capacity. After all, many children grow up with a parent who, at some point, will have some kind of mental health difficulty though these are mostly mild or short-lived, and they will usually be treated successfully by their general practitioner. In the UK, 68% of women and 57% of men with a formally diagnosed mental illness are parents and many children live with a parent who has long-term mental health problems, including alcohol or drug problems and personality disorders (Royal College of Psychiatrists 2016). This does not mean that they cannot be the primary carers of their children, as a diagnosis per se does not indicate a reduced parenting capacity: there are many parents with a distinct psychiatric diagnosis who are excellent parents and there are also plenty of parents who do not meet the criteria required for a psychiatric diagnosis whose parenting capacity is judged to be inadequate. However, the literature does suggest an *association* between parental mental health and negative outcomes for children (Rutter & Quinton 1984; Cassell & Coleman 1995; Falkov 1998; Cleaver et al. 1999; Duncan & Reder 2000; Goepfert et al 2004; Smith 2004). Thus, while it cannot be assumed that parents with a psychiatric diagnosis will inevitably have difficulties with parenting, it nevertheless constitutes a risk factor. When assessing a parent's mental health, the practitioner's main task is to ascertain whether it impacts adversely on the quality of their parenting.

Personality disorders and personality traits

In order for an experienced psychiatrist or psychologist to diagnose an individual as suffering from a personality disorder, various criteria need to be met. For example, there have to be documented impairments in personality functioning and personality trait expression and these have to be relatively stable and consistent across time and situations, and not be due to the direct effects of substance misuse or a general medical condition. Furthermore, any impairments need to be 'abnormal' in terms of the individual's developmental stage and socio-cultural environment. The domains of impaired functioning include cognition, affectivity, impulse control and interpersonal relationships. The practitioner will also examine the parent's degree of identity integration, the type of defensive positions habitually employed and the capacity for reality testing. The most common forms of personality traits or disorder suspected or encountered are narcissistic, borderline and antisocial.

Some parents have a profile of personality 'traits' that may not reach the threshold for a formal diagnosis, but which can impact significantly on their interpersonal functioning in specific situations. For example, a parent may function adequately at work, have found another partner, and may even have gone on to have more children who are all doing well, yet exhibit very problematic behaviours when faced with their ex-partner or the child(ren) from that relationship. In some individuals, personality traits, although at times prominently in evidence, are *not* inflexible. For example, these parents can be grandiose about their achievements, but they can also have a fairly balanced view of their own strengths and weaknesses. They can seem to lack empathy at times, for example in relation to their child(ren)'s mother or father, but be more than able to show empathy to their new partner, as well as empathizing with their children and their predicament/s. There are also parents who at times display a sense of entitlement and a lack of sensitivity to the needs and wants of others, but this may not be a pervasive pattern. They may sometimes be oblivious to the hurt their remarks inflict on others, but at other times they can display good sensitivity and subsequently reflect on their conduct in a self-critical way. And there are those parents who can display, perhaps frequently, seemingly arrogant, disdainful, condescending or patronizing attitudes and behaviours, but on other occasions the very same parent can show some humility and diffidence. Antisocial traits include impulsive, irresponsible and often criminal behaviours, as well as being manipulative, deceitful and reckless. In summary, all the above listed personality traits can be context specific and may manifest themselves less in +parent's relations with their child(ren) than they do when the parent is interacting with the other parent and/or professionals. Personality traits have a tendency to become more marked when the person feels stressed and/or distressed, and this is particularly the case in entrenched parental disputes which can drive not only the parents but also others quite literally 'mad'.

A formal diagnosis of mental illness or disorder can only ever be a shorthand description, with rather limited explanatory power or relevance. The practitioner's main focus should be on understanding how personality features, be those traits or actual disorders, may impact on parenting and the welfare of children. This informs the recommended evidence-based treatment options, if any, and whether or not sufficient improvements in the parent's mental health can happen within timescales that are compatible with the child's needs (Asen & Schuff 2003).

Narcissistic traits and narcissistic personality disorder

To make the diagnosis of narcissistic personality disorder (NPD), there have to be impairments in self-functioning (e.g. difficulties with self-esteem and emotional regulation) *and* interpersonal functioning (e.g. difficulties with empathy and intimacy). In addition, one would expect to see the presence of specific pathological personality traits, such as attention seeking and grandiosity. Individuals with a narcissistic personality often refer to – and exaggerate – their personal talents and achievements and they tend to have an inflated sense of self-importance. They are rarely able to sustain close and intimate relationships over time and may present with emotional and dramatic behaviours when they feel criticized or rejected. Individuals with narcissistic personality traits have a heightened sense of self-worth which often conceals an underlying fragile self-esteem. They may excessively denigrate and criticize others, which may well be an often unconscious mechanism designed to boost their own self-esteem.

Some parents diagnosed with narcissistic traits or a full-blown NPD make allegations and accusations against those who they experience as not agreeing with them. This grandiosity can take the form of, for example, defying court orders or refusing to accept the Finding of Fact made by a court. A parent with narcissistic traits can also be very convincing when recounting their version of events and this can lead to professionals siding with them. Indeed, when these traits are pervasive, the cost to their sense of self in having to give up their stance is so intense that they hold onto beliefs with genuine conviction, unable to engage in any form of reality testing. A fragile and brittle sense of self leads the person to experience any challenge of their views or perceptions as an attack to which they will respond vehemently, becoming enraged and making counter-accusations, with a well-developed capacity to dramatize and exaggerate.

One of the main difficulties with parents presenting with narcissistic traits or NPD is a total resistance to thinking that there could be anything wrong with them, except that they tend to get stressed. These parents are often emotionally unable to put themselves into the mind of another adult or child and to empathize with, or comprehend how, another person might experience them. Furthermore, they have an expectation that the child will be of the same mind as them, and the child(ren) may feel they need to confirm the parent's sense of self-worth by, for example, making them feel needed and important.

When spurious allegations of sexual abuse against the distanced parent are made by a parent with narcissistic traits, there is frequently no sense of parental concern at repeatedly presenting a young child for intimate physical examinations – which may well, in themselves, amount to physical and emotional abuse – in pursuit of what the parent thinks is 'right' and 'true'. Whilst the parents may state that their main concern is the child's well-being, in fact the main purpose is to discredit the distanced parent. Not infrequently the parent's own personal experiences of abuse in the past can contribute to the stance of not trusting anybody else to care for their child.

Borderline features and borderline personality disorder

Claims that the ex-partner is suffering from a borderline personality disorder (BPD) or has 'borderline features' are increasingly common when parents seek ammunition for winning a protracted court battle. The term 'borderline' is frequently, liberally and often inappropriately used in order to pathologize and disqualify the other parent. Typically this can concern any seemingly impulsive behaviours the ex-partner has demonstrated, including becoming 'emotional' when disagreeing or shouting loudly when not feeling heard or listened to. This may lead a parent to google 'borderline' and tick off a list of features and common presentations (see Box 5.2). It is important to note that the making of a formal diagnosis of BPD is a complex task and requires a certain number of specific criteria to be met (see, for example, DSM-5 2013). The practitioner's task is to verify whether any of these actually are present and, if so, determine whether or how these might impact adversely on the child's welfare.

Box 5.2 Borderline features and common presentations

Features

- Instability of interpersonal relationships, characterized by alternating between extremes of idealization and devaluation
- Persistent identity disturbance with unstable self-image
- Self-damaging impulsivity (sex, binge eating, substance abuse)
- Recurring suicidal gestures and threats
- Marked reactivity of mood and frequent displays of anger
- Chronic feelings of emptiness and dissociation
- Transient, stress-related paranoid ideation.

Common presentations

- Parent locates all blame/responsibility for difficulties externally
- Parent blames the child for having 'provoked' serious physical or sexual abuse
- Parent frequently emotionally denigrates the child
- Parent uses the child for their own gratification
- Parent has sudden unpredictable negative emotional outbursts in the presence of, or directed at, the child
- Parent rapidly alternates between over-involved and distancing behaviours
- Parent oscillates between perceiving the child as either 'good' or 'bad'.

Fabricated or induced illnesses

The intentional production of physical or psychological signs or symptoms by a primary carer in a child is an occasional feature of entrenched contact and residence disputes. Fabricated or induced illnesses (FII) – previously known as 'Munchausen syndrome by proxy' – refers to a scenario where a caregiver elicits unnecessary health care on the child(ren)'s behalf, attempting to simulate an illness by providing a false history or by fabricating evidence. This can be used in court battles when the closer parent claims that the child is too ill to be cared for by the other parent. Typically, the parent seeks to persuade everyone that their child is physically unwell when there is no evidence of it, or when the parent exaggerates or lies about their child's symptoms. This can severely limit the child's daily life and activities and, intentionally or inadvertently, lead to a cessation of contact with the distanced parent. If the latter makes objections to the child being treated medically, these are dismissed by the closer parent and interpreted as signs that the distanced parent simply does not care.

Anxiety, depression and responses to trauma

Chronic inter-parental conflict can have an impact on a parent's mental health, with low mood and anxiety states being the most common sequelae. However, anxiety and depression can pre-date the conflicts and parental separation. When this is the case, it may be used to support allegations of poor parenting. Anxiety and depression can affect a parent's ability to be emotionally available to their child. In more severe cases it can affect a parent's daily functioning and ability to provide 'good enough' care. The children of parents with more severe symptoms of anxiety and/or depression can find themselves taking on caring roles, with responsibilities beyond their age, particularly when the family is also socially isolated. Often children embrace these responsibilities as it serves an attachment need in that, by providing care themselves, children maintain physical and emotional proximity to their primary caregiver. It is important to assess a parent's ability to be self-reflective in relation to their mood changes and how these impact on their own feelings, thoughts and actions and those of others, as well as their ability to put into place effective coping strategies and use social support. Parents who have not seen their children for an extended period of time and whose children are refusing to see them can respond with depression, withdrawal and passivity, shame, guilt and self-blame, anger and impatience and/or bewilderment (Goldberg & Goldberg 2013).

Questionnaires, such as the Beck Depression Inventory (Beck et al. 1996) and Beck Anxiety Inventory (Beck & Steer 1988) are not diagnostic per se, but they can provide useful snapshots of current symptomology. Often parents specify that they feel, for example, 'hopeless', but only in response to the protracted disputes. However, some parents are – and in some cases justifiably so – concerned that any disclosure of symptoms of depression and anxiety could be used against them by the other parent, and hence they under-report psychological symptoms.

Experience of trauma can have a significant impact on mental health which may extend beyond the specific symptoms of post-traumatic stress disorder (PTSD). 'Complex post-traumatic stress disorder' (CPTSD; Brewin et al. 2017) was included in the recently released ICD-11 (2018) and describes disturbances in self-organization, such as affect dysregulation, negative self-concept and interpersonal disturbances, which can sometimes result from multiple, chronic or repeated traumas from which escape is difficult or impossible. Examples are childhood abuse, domestic violence, torture and war imprisonment. It is therefore essential when assessing parents to ascertain whether there is a history of trauma and, when appropriate, to consider the impact this may have on their functioning as a caregiver to their child. In cases of established domestic violence, the practitioner conducting the assessment must be careful to avoid triggering symptoms of trauma.

When assessing parents' mental health, a useful adjunct to the clinical interview and observations and other relevant information contained in the court bundle or provided by other professionals or family members, is the use of validated psychometric measures, such as the Millon Personality Inventory (Millon & Bloom 2008). This assessment tool can provide helpful information on personality traits, mental health issues and psychopathology, as well as response tendencies. For example, respondents can be given a score indicating the level of disclosure and desirable responding. While psychometric measures can provide useful additional information, they need to be regarded as one component of a comprehensive assessment and should therefore be considered within the broader context of the referral and the different sources of information emerging during the assessment process.

Chapter 6

Therapeutic assessment of family relationships and planning interventions

Therapeutic assessments

In the Family Ties approach, the individual assessments of children and parents precede any assessment work involving the parental couple or other family relationships. Given the frequent reluctance of ex-partners to be in the same room together, preparatory work often needs to be undertaken. Similarly, children have to be carefully prepared to meet with a parent who they may not have seen for a significant amount of time.

The somewhat unusual term 'therapeutic assessment' (Asen 2007) signifies that the assessment focus is not only on observing and describing family relationships, but also on intervening in problematic interactions and helping family members to make positive changes. The parents' and other family members' ability and willingness to think and act differently can then be assessed to inform the prognosis and recommendations the practitioner is able to make. Any relevant observations made by the practitioner can be fed back, highlighting positives and areas of competence, as well as areas of concern. The aim is to put parents in a position where they can respond to feedback given by practitioners and consider making some changes to their views and actions. In this way assessment turns into a dynamic and therapeutic process, involving direct feedback, advice and therapeutic intervention from the practitioner who is then in a position to evaluate whether positive changes have taken place or will do so in the future – or not. This allows for any existing risks to the welfare of the child(ren) to be re-assessed post-intervention to determine whether the risks have increased, decreased or remained the same.

The main questions to be addressed during this phase of work are:

1. Is each parent able to focus primarily on the welfare of the child? If not, can they change?
2. Is each parent able to act on their understanding of the child's emotional needs? If not, can they change?
3. Is each parent able to participate in some form of non-conflictual co-parenting? If not, can they change?
4. Is the child able to allow contact to happen and benefit from it? If not, can the parents and child change?
5. Is the child able to have a meaningful relationship with each parent and their respective family and friendship network?

Case example

Nina's parents divorced when she was five years old. She continued to live with her mother and saw her father from time to time. When aged ten, her gymnastics teacher noticed a bruise on her arm. When asked how it happened, Nina told her teacher that her mother had lost her temper when she refused to do her homework, dragged her up the stairs to her bedroom and locked her in there. Nina said that this had happened before. It was decided that Nina should live temporarily with her father while social services were conducting their investigation. Her mother admitted the incident, but she denied that she had ever harmed her before. Nina said that she wanted to remain living with her father and refused to have any form of contact with her mother. Her father stated that Nina should not be forced to see her mother and that one should wait until she was 'ready'. The court ordered an assessment of the parents and when first seen, each parent blamed the other for the breakdown in contact. Despite their mutual accusations, both parents appeared motivated to protect Nina from their conflicts. During the course of the assessment Nina's father agreed to encourage her to have contact with her mother, but Nina continued to be very anxious at the prospect, providing seemingly authentic accounts of past emotionally and physically abusive behaviours she had suffered when in her care, whilst at the same time also acknowledging some of the positive qualities her mother had. Nina spoke about being upset when thinking about how her mother might feel as a result of her refusing contact and she said that she knew that her mother had not meant to hurt her. After viewing a video message from her mother and with her father's support, Nina agreed to meet her. Despite preparation, her mother minimized Nina's negative experiences in her care, which was met with Nina's disappointment and she told her mother that 'nothing has changed'. The mother explained Nina's reaction in terms of the father alienating Nina, though not in Nina's presence.

Preparing parents for meeting with ex-partners

Bringing warring parents together to focus on their children may initially be carried out in parallel processes. Parents will need to be helped to shift their focus away from their ex-partner's perceived negligent and/or inadequate or malicious behaviours and onto their children's welfare. This can be a major challenge and requires disentangling two potentially conflicting roles the parents have: being ex-partners and being co-parents. The latter implies that it is likely that many joint decisions about their children will need to be made for years to come and at least for the remainder of their minority.

In separate, parallel sessions each parent is asked to list their fears and hopes of meeting with their ex-partner: 'What are you most worried about when meeting him/her? And if you could allow yourself to have any hopes, what might they be? Imagine that he/she was in this room and you enter and you see each other – what would help you to make this a good meeting? What would he/she have to do or not do so that you feel comfortable? Well, let us imagine he/she is sitting in the room as you enter, what might you be thinking and feeling – and what about your ex-partner?'

This can be followed by the exploration of hypothetical scenarios, i.e. identifying a number of potentially distressing situations that could occur during a joint session with the ex-partner and thinking about to handle these. The parent can think about his/her responses and then rehearse, via mini-role plays, a number of different options, designed to avoid familiar escalations. Examples of how to begin to explore hypothetical scenarios are as follows: 'Supposing he said that and looked at you in the way that you say makes you feel very uncomfortable – how could you respond?'; or 'Supposing she raises the issue of the maintenance – which is due to be settled in the next court hearing – how might you reply or handle yourself? Let us imagine that I am your ex-partner and I have just accused you, yet again, of brainwashing the children, how might you respond?'

The 'pattern as culprit'

The three distinct inter-parental patterns observed in high-conflict families post-separation – mutual blaming, blaming-blocking and blocking-blocking (see Chapter 1) – can be identified and addressed directly when working with parents. Naming the pattern and enlisting both parents' support to defeat it for the sake of the child 'externalizes the problem' (White 1999) and can shift the focus away from blaming the other parent to 'blaming' the pattern. The parents are encouraged to think about what each can do to reduce the problem pattern: 'You both block each other, and I am not blaming either of you for it, it is a pattern that has developed and it places your child right in the middle of it all … What can you each do to defeat that pattern? Please focus on the pattern and what you can do to not let it impact on your child.'

Each parent focusing on what they themselves can do, rather than what the other parent should do, can also be helpful in promoting change.

Managing emotional arousal by validation

Parents can become upset if not enraged when talking about the past injustices they feel they have suffered at the hands of their ex-partner. High levels of emotional arousal are usually incompatible with effective mentalizing. By referring to their own state of mind ('I cannot think clearly if you shout'), the practitioner can pause the aroused parent and buy time to get their mentalizing capacity back 'online' rather than attempting to rationally 'understand' the parent, let alone ask why he/she is so angry. This simple move can stimulate reflective contemplation in both parent and practitioner. When a parent's capacity to mentalize is temporarily compromised due to high affect, the recognition and validation of this very state of mind is necessary to help the parent down-regulate their emotional state. Similarly, when a parent presents strongly held beliefs that are resistant to any rational challenges and seem to have an almost delusional quality, the practitioner can refer to these as 'your truth' rather than questioning or, worse, dismissing them. Validating a parent's conviction in this way also reduces the shame or anger associated with being considered a liar or being simply 'wrong'. Similarly, validating a parent's stance that it is not his/her intention to triangulate their child can also have a calming effect. When, in a state of high emotional arousal, a parent usually loses sight of the child, the practitioner may shift the focus: 'I am just remembering that my job is to think about your child's experience ... what sense do you think she would make of this view you have? Would this be appropriate? If not, how should it be different? How can we both work towards that?' Shifting the balance of attention onto the child can help a parent regain the capacity to mentalize. With children, the task of managing high arousal is somewhat more complex. While it is equally important to validate the child's emotional experience, the practitioner needs to be especially careful not to validate an inaccurate narrative, for example that a parent sexually abused a child when this has been found not to be true. In these instances the practitioner may tell the child: 'I read that this is not what the judge found, but I can hear strongly that you are saying something different and telling me that your parent did the wrong thing'.

Recognizing and validating the parent's emotional experience can often be a rather complex task. For example, it is not at all uncommon for parents to vent their anger and frustration at the practitioner for not being able to quickly and directly 'fix the problem', accompanied by raging at the perceived injustice inflicted by a seemingly incompetent and uncaring family court system. This may well camouflage the paralysing shame of being rejected by one's own child and the practitioner needs to be aware and tolerant of these dynamics in order to enable the parent to feel listened to and encouraged to open up more.

Preparing parents for re-establishing contact with their child

When parents have not seen their child(ren) for many months or even years, it is usually very difficult for them to envisage a first encounter. They understandably feel that they no longer know their child, not least because they may only have had sparse accounts of the child's interests, friendships and social activities. If the distanced parent has seen their child more recently, the encounters may have been brief and characterized by the child's negativity and/or by the attitude of the resident parent who perhaps was present during those contacts and felt forced to facilitate them. Distanced parents often say that they don't know what to expect and they almost inevitably blame the closer parent for withholding essential information about their child(ren). The practitioner can refocus the closer parent on what it might be like for the child having to see the distanced parent. The 'I don't know' response can be countered by asking the parent to imagine '*a* child, not *your* child, *a* child who has not seen his/her mother or father for a long time – what do you think might be going on in that child's mind? And what might that child think or feel about the parent he/she lives with who they know literally cannot stand the other parent?'

Putting the parent in a reflective position in relation to a hypothetical 'other child' can stimulate mentalizing processes that may initially not work for their own child – a hypothetical scenario is usually not emotionally loaded. Similarly, putting the parent into the position of mentalizing both parents of a hypothetical child may build a bridge to eventually considering their own states of mind, allowing them to begin to talk about their own personal fears and hopes and how these may be managed in anticipation of the child's first encounter with the distanced parent. Whether and how parents use this support provides an indication of their capacity and willingness to mentalize their child and themselves: it is part of the assessment of their ability to engage with interventions, and informs opinions and decisions with regard to the viability and form of any further therapeutic work.

Preparing children for re-establishing contact with their parent

The Family Ties approach aims to give parents the primary responsibility for preparing the child for contact with the distanced parent. The practitioner assists by emphasizing the importance of contact and highlights the potentially negative impact on children of having no direct contact with one of their parents. Available research evidence, as detailed in Chapters 1 and 2, can be pointed to, followed by winding the clock forward, so to speak, and getting the parent to think about what it might be like for their child to grow up with a negative representation of their absent parent – for example when the 'child' is 15, 20 or 30 years old. This task demands that parents separate their child's imagined thoughts, feelings and intentions from their own. Parents are also helped to consider their child's complex feelings arising from the refusal to have any form of contact with the distanced parent – such as feelings of anger, abandonment and guilt – and the potential long-term impact of such feelings if they are sustained. Parents are asked to reflect on whether safe contact with the distanced parent might provide an opportunity for their child to experience some resolution of these feelings by, for example, experiencing first-hand that they have not been abandoned or altogether rejected by the absent parent. For some closer parents, the fear of losing the child to the other parent can produce huge anxieties and block considering the reinstatement of direct contact. Recognition of this parent's likely emotional experiences has to precede any challenging of fixed beliefs and seemingly obstructive behaviours. When a closer parent is mistrustful of the proposed direct contact work and concerned about the child's safety, the practitioner can address these anxieties by identifying, together with the parent, ways of ensuring that contact is a safe experience for the child. This can involve establishing rules for contact in advance which will have to be agreed by *both* parents. These may include close supervision of contact, phased arrival and departure of the parties at the contact centre and regular breaks during contact sessions. Here, therapeutic assessments help to identify potential barriers to the re-introduction of contact with the distanced parent and the type of intervention likely to be required to enable progression of contact.

It is not at all uncommon for parents to explicitly make it the practitioner's task to convince the child to have contact with the distanced parent. As such a request tends to meet the ambivalence of the closer parent about the desirability of contact, it is unlikely to work. Children are often suspicious of professionals and in cases where contact has been resisted, they may well align the practitioner with the distanced parent who, they believe, pressurizes them to have contact against their wishes. It is important for the practitioner to resist taking this position and instead focus on intervening in ways that support the closer parent to promote contact directly. As a first step, the child can be asked to imagine what that parent feels about the proposed contact: 'What do you imagine goes on in your dad's head when we talk about you having contact with your mum? If you could hear his thoughts, what might you be hearing?' The child's guesswork can be checked with the parent who may, or may not, agree with the child. When a child responds with 'I don't know', the practitioner can playfully construct with the child a 'mind scanner' (Asen & Fonagy 2012b) on a piece of paper which the practitioner holds over his/her own head before embarking on doing so with a parent: 'Look at this head … my head … what do you think I am thinking this very second? Look at my face, look at my eyes, try to figure out what goes on in there … and now put the mind scanner over your dad's head – what might be going on in there?'

Assessing the parental couple relationship

When parents are from the outset both willing and able to meet together in the same room with the practitioner, their current relationship as co-parents can be assessed 'in vivo'. Some of the most common general themes addressed in joint parental couple assessment sessions are listed in Box 6.1.

Box 6.1 Areas and themes of the joint parental couple assessment

- Mutual trust and respect
- Managing disagreements and problem solving
- Ability to question and challenge each other without escalation
- Managing stress
- Ability to mentalize self and ex-partner
- Willingness/ability to make joint decisions
- Ability to recognize the impact of inter-parental hostility on their child
- Ability to protect the child(ren) from inter-parental hostility
- Managing different cultural expectations.

The focus of the parental couple sessions depends largely on the severity and chronicity of the parental conflict. In less severe cases, when contact is often still in place and the child spends significant amounts of time with *both* parents, the parental couple may find communicating with each other stressful, but nonetheless manage to do so. In these cases it is important to have a clear agenda for the joint parental couple sessions, mutually agreed by both parents prior to the session, for example via an exchange of emails into which the practitioner is copied. The agenda needs to focus on parenting arrangements and issues likely to arise in the immediate future.

When inter-parental conflict is more severe, a very structured approach is required, with the basic rules for conduct being explained to each parent prior to the first session and repeated at the beginning of each subsequent one. The rules are there to provide a safe space for focusing on the needs of the child(ren): the practitioner explains that the session is going to be tightly chaired, with equal space and time given for each parent and that the parents interrupting each other will not be tolerated. Each parent is asked to submit an agenda of topics for discussion, concerning only potential co-parenting issues. The practitioner also explains that the session will be stopped if the emotional arousal of one or both parents is high, with a brief pause being suggested for 'cooling down' or, if this is not sufficient for the arousal to be lowered, termination of the session. Once each parent has submitted their respective agenda items, agreement is sought and reached on which item to start with. Parents are requested to take it in turn to present an item and neither can talk for longer than 2 minutes at a time; this requires the other parent to listen and not interrupt the speaker, although they may take notes in order to remember points that they wish to raise subsequently. When talking, each parent is asked to look only at the practitioner and direct all questions or answers to the practitioner and not to the ex-partner. Any comments that criticize or blame the other parent are immediately stopped by the practitioner who explains that these are unacceptable and that, if these continue, the session will have to be terminated. The practitioner's firm and boundaried stance is essential for these meetings to succeed. If the levels of arousal and hostility are very intense, the session can be continued in two separate rooms, with the practitioner literally 'shuttling' between the warring parents, relaying child-focused messages from one parent to the other and back. The practitioner may, after a series of increasingly breathless 'shuttles', comment on how he/she can understand their child's position and what it is like to be in the role of a 'go-between', 'diplomat' or 'peace maker'. Not infrequently parents then agree to reconvene in the same room and change their conduct.

Various topics can be discussed during a parental couple session. Contact handover arrangements are a frequent subject and the practitioner can, for example, focus the discussion as follows: 'When the contact handover takes place outside the supermarket and you, the parents, don't greet each other – how do you think your children are affected? What might they think at that moment? And when their father telephones them at your home, how could you communicate to them that you welcome this?' The practitioner may encourage the parents in a quickly improvised mini-role play to put themselves in the position of their child. Brief 'enactments' (Minuchin 1974) of this nature evoke likely real-life situations under controlled conditions and make a child's dilemma come alive in the room. It also permits pausing the role play to consider what might be going on in a child's mind at such a point, then possibly rewinding the interactions for further reflection. This can then be followed by another 'take': what could the parents do differently so that the child is less distressed? This allows the possibility for different, and perhaps less stressful, ways of managing contact handover or other situations.

Assessing child–parent interactions

Observing and assessing the interactions between the child(ren) and each parent starts the moment the practitioner meets a parent and child(ren) in the waiting room or wherever the first encounter takes place. Informal observations by the receptionist can be welcome sources of information: how the parent settles and prepares the child for the meeting; how the parent allows the child to roam around in the waiting room; whether and how the parent enforces any boundaries. It is also important to observe how the child separates from the parent and how the separation is explained to the child. The practitioner may encourage this explicitly, by stating: 'Can you please explain to your child that he/she is now going to see me on his/her own?' and then observe how a parent communicates this to the child.

It is usually more difficult to observe spontaneous child–parent interactions during formal assessment sessions in a clinical setting, particularly if a question and answer format is being employed by the practitioner or if everyone is on their 'best behaviour'. In order to observe 'typical' communication and relationship patterns between family members, one can actively create scenarios that encourage 'live' interactions and enactments. There are a number of tasks that families can be set to stimulate live family interaction (see Box 6.2), though these need to be tailored to the child(ren)'s age(s).

Box 6.2 Ideas for generating 'live' samples of parent–child interactions

- Here are a few bricks – why don't you all together build something with them in the next 10 minutes?
- Here is a board game – play it, I will just sit back and watch
- Talk about the likes and dislikes of each family member
- Make a plan for an outing next Sunday

- Remember the last argument between you, how it started and how it escalated. Discuss the same issues now!
- Your child is not doing what you want him/her to do. Is that OK? No? So, what are you going to do about it?
- Your child is being really well behaved right now. What would you have to say or do in order for him/her to show the sorts of problems that have brought you here?
- Together make a picture of you as a family
- Draw up the 'Ten Commandments'/the five most important rules of family life
- Discuss what the rules are about your children's use of the computer/games
- Let me see what happens around mealtimes in your family
- Get your child to do some school homework
- Pretend that the children are the parents and the parents are the children (role inversion) – now play a typical scene from family life
- Explain to your child what's 'safe' (a good or bad touch) and discuss it together
- Talk, as a family, about a really good time you had together
- Explain to your child why you have come here and that he/she has to see me on his/her own for a short time.

Various structured assessments of parent–child interactions have been proposed (e.g. Barnard & Kelly 1990; DiPasquale 2000; Aspland & Gardner 2003). The Marschak Interaction Method (MIM), for example, assesses a carer's ability to structure, engage, nurture and challenge a child via a series of structured tasks, and it evaluates the child's ability to respond to the carer's efforts (Lindaman et al. 2000). A recently introduced interaction-based measure, the Squiggle Assessment (Ensink et al. 2017), identifies three dimensions of reflective parenting: (1) interest in the subjectivity of the child, (2) affective communication and (3) the capacity to play, rated on a nine-point scale.

Observing how the closer parent talks to the child about the other parent is another major area of assessment. Invitations such as: 'Can you explain to your child why you think it is important that he/she has contact with his/her father … tell your child what his strengths are'. Parents need to be informed ahead of meeting with the child that these and related questions may be asked. Similarly, the distanced parent will be asked to talk to the child about the positive aspects of the closer parent. Observing the tone and choice of words, as well as non-verbal cues and the child's responses, including challenging the parent, all help to assemble a nuanced picture of parent–child interactions. The parent's ability to hold onto and put into action preparatory work that has been carried out prior to the session also provides valuable information about their willingness and capacity to consider changing their approach.

It is often important to also formally assess the sibling relationships (Box 6.3), particularly when there is a question as to whether or not siblings should have different levels of contact with the distanced parent or where they should live.

Box 6.3 Areas for the assessment of sibling relationships

- Attachments and other characteristics of the inter-sibling relationships
- Levels of inter-sibling emotional and physical conflicts
- Positioning of each sibling in relation to each parent (including different experiences of abuse and/or neglect) and its effects on the sibling relationship
- Differences in ages and, often arising from this, the needs of each sibling
- Parental roles and responsibilities of each sibling.

The wider system: extended family and culture

Frequently members of each parent's family of origin become actively involved in what has been described as 'relational war' (Van Lawick & Visser 2015). This can also draw in new partners and their family, as well as neighbours and friends, school/workmates and professionals. Members of the wider family and friendship network often take sides with one of the parents whom they see as the victim of the other parent's unreasonableness, if not malevolence. Network meetings (see Chapter 3) are an excellent opportunity to connect members of the wider system and identify their potential for helping to focus on the needs of the child(ren).

When working with parents and children, knowledge and understanding of different cultural systems and customs, such as kinship patterns and parenting practices, is important. Furthermore, the range of different 'sub-cultures' – groupings of people in the same society who are viewed differently from the parent culture in which they are embedded – adds another layer of complexity. There are also families which do not have a strong identification with their ancestral heritage and instead opt for identities based on religion, secular urbanity or a combination of cross-cultural influences. Whatever the family's 'culture', be that its actual values, beliefs and customs, this is often only viewed in terms of its ethnicity and its conduct is observed through an implicit lens of expectation (Connolly et al. 2006). In this way families are at risk of being reduced to being merely a cultural 'other', and their more relevant identities, based on class or faith for example, may be overlooked.

A strong sense of cultural history, traditions and customs assists children in building a positive identity for themselves and can provide a sense of belonging that is important for their mental health (Raman 2006). However, belonging to and practising different religions can prove to be a major focal point for inter-parental conflicts. When a child's parents come from different cultural and ethnic backgrounds and/or when they have different faiths, issues relating to the child's cultural identity needs and how these can be met post-separation tend to emerge. Children can experience 'cultural conflict' if they think that they have to choose one culture over the other, perhaps out of loyalty to the closer parent. Rejecting one of their parents' cultural heritage can have a high price for the child in terms of disowning an important aspect of their identity. Assessing a child's cultural needs and how and whether these are being met is an important task during each assessment and not only in cases when the family subscribes to a particular faith.

Assessing a parent's flexibility or even tolerance in relation to the other parent's belief system(s) is an important task. Religious tolerance and flexibility can be a major issue in the scenario of a child having been brought up in an exclusive ultraorthodox community – be that Jewish, Muslim or Christian – when one parent decides to leave that community. The consequences for dependent children can be huge when the departing parent is demonized by the whole community. In these instances, children become intensely aware of the whole community's negative views about their loved parent which may be accompanied by the daily denigration of that parent, directly or indirectly, by their faith-based school. Often the community demands that all contact between the child and the parent ceases and, when this occurs, religion appears to trump the best interests of the child, which is to have a good relationship with *both* parents.

Integrating assessment findings and planning therapeutic intervention

While assessment and case formulation should be continuous and recursive processes, there are certain points at which the work needs to be more formally reviewed so that decisions can be made about next steps, be that more detailed assessments and/or therapeutic interventions. The Family Ties approach builds in regular feedback and review meetings, with a written summary following initial assessment provided to both parents and also any directly involved professionals. Pulling together information across different contexts is essential in understanding triangulation processes; for example, a parent may able to engage in excellent mentalizing interactions with their child until the topic of the other parent comes up; a child may be highly anxious and clingy at the prospect of contact with a distanced parent at the clinic, but will go willingly with the same parent when collected from school; a child may be able to recount good times with a distanced parent as long as their sibling is not present.

When making decisions about therapeutic intervention, there are three main questions that need to be addressed:

1. To what extent is the child involved in harmful triangulation processes as a result of the parents' conflict?
2. Is each parent able to meet the child's needs, including the need to have a relationship with both parents?
3. Can the wider system support further therapeutic interventions?

We shall consider these questions in turn and refer to the three case examples described in Chapters 1, 4 and in this chapter.

1. Involvement in child-triangulation processes

The different but overlapping triangulation processes identified in Chapter 1 can provide a useful framework for answering the following questions:

- To what extent is the child's relationship with both parents protected?
- To what extent is the child exposed to the parental conflict?
- How appropriate is the 'distance' between each child and parent?

With regard to **relationship protection**, where there is evidence of the relationship with one (or both) parent(s) being denigrated, it is important to understand this process and how it has impacted on the child's representation of the distanced parent. Rahul (see Chapter 1) started rejecting his father and his sister followed suit; their mother felt rejected and intimidated and their father felt excluded and enraged. The practitioner concluded that the mother had inadvertently influenced the children in negative ways about their father, confusing her own feeling states with those of her children. Following the assessment, the practitioner was of the view that the mother had become genuinely afraid of her ex-husband and that she was also fearful about her children's welfare when in the father's care. The practitioner concluded that this fear was largely unfounded and suggested a therapeutic intervention focused on strengthening the mother's ability to consider the long-term impact on her children of being fearful of their father and to improve her mentalizing capacity, enabling her to better prepare Rahul and Marina for future contact with their father. She had so far demonstrated an ability to use such interventions well.

By contrast, the assessment of Sarah's parents (see Chapter 4) concluded that both parents were actively denigrating each other. They had lost sight of their daughter's experiences of being triangulated by her warring parents, whose primary focus appeared to be on 'winning' their respective 'case'. The parents found it impossible to let go of the allegations they had made about each other and to help Sarah to have more appropriate relationships with both parents. The practitioner concluded that therapeutic intervention with the mother to help re-establish contact between Sarah and her father would be ineffective, and that contact between Sarah and her father should be supervised, in order to prevent him from denigrating the mother. In the case of Nina (this chapter), the practitioner concluded that the father had not fully supported the child's relationship with her mother in the past, but that during the assessment he had begun to make an effort to do so. He recognized that he had not always effectively protected Nina from his very negative feelings about his ex-wife, and appeared able to facilitate contact.

Exposure to parental conflict can inflate loyalty ties to one parent and reinforce negative messages about a distanced parent. In every case the practitioner needs to ascertain the extent of exposure and whether parents are able to move to a position where they better protect their child(ren) from their conflicts, primarily via mentalizing the impact that such exposure may have on their child. Rahul and Marina were inadvertently exposed to conflict as, for example, they saw their parents argue in the street and they witnessed their mother's distress. Both parents appeared to recognize the negative impact this had on their children, but the father also maintained that 'at least the children could see I was fighting for them'. Sarah, on the other hand, was actively involved in the conflict and was encouraged to share allegations against her father with professionals; she gained much approval and extra care from her mother for doing so. Nina had also been inadvertently exposed to some parental conflict, but both parents actively attempted to reduce any further exposure.

Examining the **appropriateness and degree of closeness/distance** of the child to each parent is another important dimension of assessment work. Factors such as the child's age, the experiences they have had with each parent and the broader family and cultural context are relevant.

In the case of Rahul and Marina (Chapter 1), the mother appeared to be overprotective of both children and in a seemingly inappropriate partnership with Rahul. Given that the children had not had any contact with their father for a long time, the physical and emotional distance between the children and their father seemed disproportionate to any harm they were likely to have experienced in his care. This contributed significantly to the distorted views they held of him. The practitioner proposed therapeutic interventions aimed at decreasing the distance and facilitating a closer relationship between the children and their father.

The relationship between Sarah and her mother (Chapter 4) was assessed as 'enmeshed', with the mother treating Sarah as a confidante and making her privy to inappropriate adult information. This unboundaried 'over-closeness' prevented any progress being made in Sarah's relationship with her father. This was particularly evident when her panic upon seeing a message from her father escalated in her mother's presence and dramatically diminished in her absence. The emotional and physical distance to her father could be partially explained as Sarah's way of managing the mismatch between her parents' opposing narratives, as well as being related to her direct experiences when in her father's care in the past. The practitioner proposed that therapeutic intervention should focus on ways of increasing the distance between her and her mother and reducing the distance between her and her father in ways that were safe considering the risk he posed.

The distance between Nina and her mother (this chapter) had increased following the disclosure of abuse and her father's position had reinforced this distance. While some distance was perhaps initially appropriate, the practitioner concluded that this was no longer helpful for Nina, and that a safe reduction of this distance was necessary for Nina to resolve some difficult feelings and to protect what was good about her relationship with her mother. However, the mother's inability to recognize the impact of some of her behaviours on her daughter meant that, for the moment, the contact was restricted.

The extent to which a child has been exposed to child triangulation processes can also be reflected in their attachment patterns, family representations and face-to-face interactions. While Rahul and Marina (Chapter 1) were angry and reluctant to see their father and largely dismissive of him, it was not hard, with their mother's help, to convince them to have direct contact with him. Sarah (Chapter 4), on the other hand, exhibited panic and a disorganized response at the prospect of seeing her father in her mother's presence, whereas Nina (this chapter) was anxious but not resistant to contact with her mother, as long as it was supervised and she could determine its frequency and duration to some extent.

2. Each parent's ability to meet the child's needs, including the need to have a relationship with both parents

In addition to understanding the type and severity of child triangulation processes, the practitioner needs to collect information about the parents' resources and capacity to protect the child from their conflict, including their ability to use support and intervention. A number of specific areas need to be assessed (see Box 6.4) to enable the practitioner to form opinions with regard to the viability of any therapeutic intervention and, if so, to plan its focus and intensity. When therapeutic intervention is contraindicated, sometimes a change of residence or placement in foster care may need to be considered.

Box 6.4 Parenting capacity dimensions

- Each parent's ability to meet their child's basic needs
- Each parent's ability to see their child and their needs through the eyes of the other parent as well as putting themselves in the 'shoes' of the child and looking at both parents from that perspective
- Each parent's ability to talk about the importance of the child having both parents in their life and to make plans to enable this, including agreeing goals for therapeutic intervention
- Each parent's ability and willingness to explore and analyse how interactional patterns of communication between them can triangulate the child and produce loyalty conflicts
- Each parent's capacity to look at how their past behaviour may have contributed to the suffering of their child(ren), including their own negative views of their ex-partner and how these may have been communicated to the child(ren), deliberately or inadvertently
- Each parent's ability and willingness to work in partnership with the other parent for the benefit of their child(ren).

3. Can the wider system support therapeutic interventions?

When practitioners recommend further therapeutic interventions, these are less likely to be successful if key members of the family and the wider system are not involved. Practitioners therefore need to form opinions as to the appropriateness of involving the wider system of the child and family, be that the new partners of each parent, members of the extended family, professionals, loyal friends, important community or religious figures. The main aim is to help parents to accept that their child has to have 'good enough' relationships not only with both parents, but also with the significant persons from each parent's family and their respective social networks.

It is frequently the case that a parent's entrenched position is supported by members of their family or by a new partner who deliberately or inadvertently contributes to the maintenance of a dysfunctional pattern. Therapeutic interventions should therefore directly involve any important 'allies' of each parent.

Chapter 7

Re-establishing and sustaining contact

One of the main characteristics of the Family Ties approach is its emphasis on helping parents to mentalize themselves, each other and their children more effectively. When children have not seen one of their parents for a long time, re-establishing and sustaining contact with the distanced parent is a major aim. Here the Family Ties approach consists of desensitizing children and gradually exposing them to the distanced parent, in parallel to the co-construction of a coherent narrative around contact and life events, in order to repair the contradictions in children's understanding of the complex situation they are in (Asen & Morris 2016).

Case example

Mr K had not seen his daughter for some five years. The mother had abducted the child to another country when she was aged five and only after involving Interpol and The Hague Convention was it possible to trace them. Arianna was aged 11 when she and her mother were extradited to the UK and the family court ordered an assessment of the child with a view of there being contact between the child and her father. Arianna was totally resistant to having any form of contact with her father, having been told by her mother that her father was a pervert and had sexually abused her when she was a small child – despite the court having found some five years earlier that there was no substance to these allegations. When beginning the therapeutic work, the father was asked to consider providing a brief video message for Arianna. He did this with a lot of imagination, using objects and cards Arianna had made for him as a young child in an attempt to trigger some positive memories in his daughter. The mother was asked to view the video message and she thought it was 'OK' for Arianna to watch it. However, Arianna closed her eyes and put her fingers in her ears, pretending not to listen. She became upset and challenged the practitioners, asking 'why should I watch this message from this man who abused me?! He is a liar and a pervert!' She seated herself on her mother's lap and buried her head in her mother's chest. With the practitioners' encouragement the mother repeatedly asked Arianna to watch and listen to the message, reassuring her of her safety, and she eventually complied. Work then started to prepare Arianna and the father for the first direct face-to-face contact, including providing a coherent jointly constructed narrative for Arianna explaining the rationale for contact, including that her father was not a danger to her. It started with her 'spying' her father from a long distance with binoculars and this eventually resulted in them being in the same room together. Progress was slow and the father's huge patience eventually paid off and Arianna began to talk to her father, initially in rather challenging ways. All contacts between Arianna and her father took place in the presence of the practitioners and the mother said that as long as contacts were supervised by a trustworthy person, she would be OK with it. She eventually agreed that the paternal grandmother, with whom Arianna had had a very good relationship prior to being prevented from seeing her father, could fulfil this role. Contacts were gradually moved out of the clinical setting and began taking place in cafes and shopping centres and they were eventually moved to the father's home. Nine months had passed since therapeutic work had first started and father and daughter were now very relaxed in each other's company. Arianna also met the father's new wife and her two step-sisters. Some months later the practitioners proposed joint meetings for the parents to build on the coherent narrative that had already begun to form, explaining to Arianna the circumstances of her early life. It took four meetings to achieve this and eventually Arianna joined her parents to hear them both deliver the narrative together.

Desensitization and graded exposure work

Typically, graded exposure to the distanced parent takes place over a fairly short period of time (about 4–6 weeks) with tightly spaced consecutive sessions. The rationale for the desensitization work has to be explained to both the parents and the wider system around the child. It is important to check with independent sources, such as the children's schools, about how they are on the days following contact. The child's views regarding the rate of graded exposure need to be taken into account in these cases (Fidler & Bala 2013) and inform the future pace and nature of further work. In cases presenting with chronic triangulating processes and where the closer parents are thought to be actively undermining contact, focused work needs to take place with them before real progress can be made (Garber 2011b). If it is then found that the closer parent is unable to support contact, the responsibility for bringing the child to contact can be handed to another family member or a professional, but only if there is confidence that the contact is not subsequently being undermined by the closer parent and/or members of his/her family. This usually becomes evident when there is an obvious lack of progress with contact and/or when the parent claims that contact is causing emotional harm to the child, affecting both the child's health and performance at school. Evidence for any such claims may need to be sought from the GP or school. In extreme cases the practitioner may need to indicate to the resident parent that if no progress is made, a recommendation will be made to the court to remove the child from the resident parent's care and place the child either with the other parent or in a bridging foster placement on a short-term basis. In most cases, once a child is placed away, exposure to the distanced parent can normally progress more quickly, though often at the cost of considerable upheaval in the child's life. Similarly, if a distanced parent is unable to make contact a beneficial experience for the child, for example by getting into disputes with the child about specific events and being unable to use guidance to improve matters, a re-assessment of the child's contact needs may have to be considered.

Indirect graded exposure

When contact with the distanced parent has not happened for a long time, the first stage of work is indirect graded exposure to the distanced parent via a short audio-visual message. This is prepared with the help of the practitioner, possibly with relevant information about the child's current interests supplied by the closer parent. This can also send a message to the child that the parents are communicating with each other. Reference to good times in the past can be used to challenge the idea that there had never been any good experiences for the child with the distanced parent. References to favourite childhood toys and other objects may demonstrate to the child that the parent has kept him/her in mind while further prompting procedural memory about positive memories and experiences with that parent. Reassurances can be given to the child that the parent is not angry with him/her for refusing to have contact in order to help the child with likely feelings of guilt and a misplaced sense of responsibility. The type of questions asked by the distanced parent can demonstrate a wish to know more and may form the basis for a first, safe dialogue.

The closer parent is shown the audio-visual message prepared by the distanced parent without the child in the first instance and will be asked whether they approve the message. If suggestions for changes are made, these can be relayed to the other parent. If the audio-visual message is deemed to be acceptable, it becomes the closer parent's responsibility to prepare the child for viewing the clip. The practitioner will ask the resident parent to imagine the child's responses and how these should or could be handled, for example if the child refuses to watch the video or panics, cries, screams and runs out of the room. Mini-role plays might assist in getting the parent to prepare for all likely responses so that when the child views the clip the parent is prepared for all eventualities and has some concrete strategies in mind. When the child actually comes to watch the message, this is best done in the presence of the practitioner. It can be viewed by the child and closer parent once and then be watched again a second time, and the child then has the opportunity to comment or ask questions. Sometimes children watch the message again at home and may record a message for the distanced parent. This is relayed by the practitioner, who helps the distanced parent prepare a response, even if the child's message appears to be accusatory or rejecting.

Graded direct exposure

In line with the approach of graded exposure to the 'feared object' – i.e. the distanced parent – the next stage involves some form of direct contact, but initially from a distance. This is planned well in advance, with the child and resident parent's input as to what form the contact should take, so that both can feel that their anxieties have been validated and also that any possible fears are reduced by being given some control over the process. Anxieties can be further diminished by addressing practicalities, such as the order in which each parent will arrive and leave so as not to have any chance encounters along the way or in the waiting room.

To begin with it may be appropriate to view the parent from a distance. One way to do this is to use binoculars through which the estranged parent – in the street, in a garden, in a park – can be spied. The child is told that the distanced parent is aware of being watched, but that the parent won't look back at the child or wave unless instructed. This allows the child time to study the parent from a safe distance first. The use of a one-way mirror, if available, can be another useful desensitization tool that can be employed to view a parent from a distance (Weitzman 2013).

A decision needs to be made in advance as to whether or not the closer parent is present during this phase. This will depend on their ability and willingness to facilitate contact and how much parental support and management the child is likely to need. In some instances it can be beneficial for a closer parent to be present to witness the first contact and obtain a direct experience of the other parent not being abusive but sensitive to the child's needs, and also to see their child being comfortable and contained in the distanced parent's presence. These experiences can later be referred to in order to challenge the child's possible claims that contact had been very negative. There are also occasions when children outright refuse contact unless their closer parent is present. It is for this reason that, alongside a gradual increase in the child's exposure to the distanced parent, the approach involves a parallel gradual reduction of the closer parent's presence during contact: they can, for example, sit increasingly further away from their child, reading a book and/or leaving the room briefly to make a telephone call or go to the bathroom. The presence of the closer parent during first contacts can be beneficial as it allows children to concretely experience that their parents can be together in the same room and behave civilly towards one another.

Most children are curious about the distanced parent's life, but find it difficult to express this openly. The practitioner can become the 'voice of the child' and ask the type of questions that the child might want to know the answers to, such as 'What do you do for a job?' or 'How is granny?' Improved communication between child and parent is further developed when the practitioner asks the child to feed the distanced parent some interesting questions. The child may whisper a series of questions to the practitioner, who then repeats these and thereby literally amplifies the child's voice. Soon the child may ask the questions directly, making the practitioner's amplification unnecessary. For some children there is no conversation to be had other than one which directly challenges the distanced parent, for example: 'Why were you so mean to mummy?' or 'Why did you always shout at us?' As questions of this nature need to be anticipated, the distanced parent could be pre-prepared, in mini role-plays, to answer these questions in a calm manner. Suggested wordings could be: 'I don't think we should talk about the past, it is sad what happened in the past and I am really sorry that you were around to see it ... and I promise I won't shout at you, there is no reason to shout at you, you are such a nice child'.

Playfulness and humour can lighten the atmosphere and be used as a tool when mentalizing goes 'offline'. For example, when a child is strongly resisting contact with the distanced parent, the practitioner can engage in a playful interaction, such as joining the child in hiding under a table or becoming seemingly exhausted and dramatically out of breath from running backwards and forwards from child to parent across a room, or from the consulting room to the road or garden outside where the distanced parent may be placed.

Reducing anxieties

When undertaking this work, it is essential to prepare the closer parent to manage their child's anxiety and resistance to encountering the distanced parent, with a clear safeguarding policy in place (see Chapter 8). It is important not to terminate the graded exposure work while the child is still anxious as this reinforces the recursive process of anxiety leading to avoidance and lack of exposure to the 'feared object' – the distanced parent – which leads to further avoidance. The focus of these first contact meetings is considered and decided by the parents and it is important not to spend too much time negotiating with the child about what the focus should be or listening to the seemingly endless grievances held by the child. Photos and memories can be shared, games played and videos or films watched. A child may still be largely rejecting of their parent, but nevertheless be able to remain in their presence and have a somewhat positive – or at least not a negative – experience. Parents are encouraged to respond in light-hearted ways during contact and it is afterwards that they may need to be helped to manage their feelings of rejection and to come to a better understanding of how their child might receive the message that they continue to love them despite their rejecting behaviour. Once a child is able to be in the same room with the previously feared parent without becoming distressed, the duration and frequency of contact can be increased and even be moved out of the clinical setting, such as going for a meal to a restaurant, which can be a normalizing experience and freeing for both parent and child. In this scenario the practitioner remains present during contact but takes as much of a back seat as possible. If assessed as safe and agreed with both parents and the child, the practitioner may leave the distanced parent alone with the child for brief periods of time, challenging the often expressed view that the parent 'is only being nice because you are there'. A further progression of direct face-to-face contact can be supported by in-between indirect contact, e.g. via Skype or text messages, as agreed with the closer parent and monitored if necessary.

In cases where contact between a child and a distanced parent is ongoing but has deteriorated in quality and/or frequency, graded exposure to that parent – as described above – is not necessary. However, the coordination of both parents and the wider system to support a more positive experience of contact is just as important, including challenging a child's stubborn resistance to contact and the child's avoidance of the distanced parent by postponing or stopping contacts altogether. For example, if a child repeatedly becomes distressed during contact and wants to go home after just a few minutes for no apparent reason, the parents are supported to work together to enable the child to stay for longer periods of time. This allows the child to experience their parents working together to support contact.

Challenging distorted representations

Contact with the distanced parent provides an opportunity to test the child's fears and criticisms in vivo. In line with cognitive and behavioural approaches to anxiety management, the child and the closer parent are asked to make specific predictions about how the distanced parent is likely to behave, imagining and describing in some detail how that parent will sound and look. This is followed, after contact, by questions about whether the predictions had come true: 'Did you see your father be horrible to your mother – how did he treat her?' and 'How did he treat you?' and 'Did you hear him say sorry for what he had done?' When a child attempts to disqualify what happened, it is important not to get into a battle, but merely to stay with observable facts and enlist the closer parent's support to back these up. Video recordings of a previous contact session can be viewed and re-viewed and this method may challenge the often selective or even distorted memories and representations. Such feedback can also continue between meetings, via text or Skype where appropriate.

When there have been examples in contact sessions of a parent being sarcastic or angry, work with the parent to think about the impact of that experience on their child and the quality of contact that is required. This will potentially allow the child to have a better experience during the next contact session. In cases where contact is ongoing but strained and in danger of breaking down, a common complaint of children is that the distanced parent is, or has been, 'too strict'. The provision of consistency via a parenting agreement (see Chapter 9) can address any real or potential discrepancies between parenting practices in relation to rules and boundaries.

Re-scripting

Children caught up in their parents' acrimonious relationship are usually not in a position to develop a consistent and coherent narrative about their family circumstances and why they are only having limited or no contact with one of their parents. This is typically because they have been receiving conflicting narratives from what have once been trusted sources of information – their parents. This experience is painful and overwhelming and can produce confusion and loyalty conflicts. When distressed, children are likely to turn to the parent they live with as the most reliable informant about the past. This makes it difficult for children to challenge the narrative and beliefs of that parent as it poses an anxiety to children that they may risk losing both parents. Children's seemingly determined adherence to the distorted family narrative therefore seems a matter of physical and psychological survival and explains why they can appear invested in their denial of anything 'good', both past and present, about the distanced parent, or, in more extreme cases, in making and upholding allegations of parental abuse and neglect. This stance protects the child from possible inner turmoil arising from the conflicting narratives and cements the alignment with the closer parent. However, it comes with the cost of increasing the distance between the child and their other parent.

The conviction with which some children appear to hold their often negative if not demonizing views and beliefs about the absent parent, and the associated distress and attachment behaviours they display at the prospect of any form of contact with that parent, can leave practitioners questioning their own narrative: not infrequently they begin to wonder whether the allegations may, after all, be true and worry that insisting that the child resumes contact could itself be an act of 'professional abuse' or a deplorable collusion with an abusive parent. When this happens practitioners sometimes need to remind themselves why establishing face-to-face contact is important for children who find themselves in this situation, allowing them to 'reality test', as it were, their views of the distanced parent's alleged shortcomings and correcting the frightening and negative images they have built up in their minds. This provides children with the opportunity to obtain reassurance that they have not harmed the rejected parent, that this parent continues to love them, that this parent is not angry with them and, when appropriate and possible, to gain some resolution of the grievances they hold. Where possible, it is equally important for children to gain reassurances that contact with the distanced parent will not damage the relationship they have with the closer parent.

Re-scripting refers to the construction of a coherent narrative involving both parents, separately first and hopefully jointly at some stage, explaining why contact should take place and taking into account the closer parent's previous objections. The narrative also needs to address any unsubstantiated allegations as well actual past negative experiences the child has had with the distanced parent. The short-term aim of constructing the script is to reduce the stress on the child of holding two or more conflicting realities in their minds and the pressure of having to choose between them. The long-term benefit is the likelihood that a coherent narrative will benefit the child's developing sense of self (Morris & Asen 2018). However, as far as the parents are concerned, this tends to be a difficult task as it is likely to challenge and unbalance firmly held views, not only of the parents but also the wider system, be that members of the extended family or friends and professionals. In addition, Findings of Fact made by the court further complicate matters if one or both parents do not accept these.

Re-scripting work is likely to cause temporary anxieties as to how the child may respond to a new narrative. While it is essential not to deny or minimize any negative or abusive experience a child may have had with the distanced parent, a major task in helping the child move towards having contact is to connect with more positive memories of the distanced parent. Sadly it is often the case that the child has lost all recollection of such memories, displacing or literally forgetting them. The number of positive interactions a child has had with the distanced parent varies from case to case, but almost always there will have been some positive experiences. Uncovering these when there is a flat denial on the part of the closer parent and child can be facilitated by looking at old photos and videos, for example of family holidays. This can be hard work as children often counteract any positive experiences depicted by making broad statements such as 'that was the holiday when my father told me to smile at the camera and pretend that I was happy' or 'my mother forced me swim on that holiday by throwing me in at the deep end, I nearly drowned'.

In cases of a historically very poor relationship between a child and a (now) distanced parent, contact may be primarily pursued for identity purposes rather than for building a close relationship. Here it might be more congruent with the child's experience to focus on 'OK and not negative' rather than 'positive' memories, at least in the first instance.

It is just as important to work with both parents to ensure they protect their children from ongoing negative messages about the other parent as it is to help them reconnect their children with positive memories. Negative messages can be either direct or indirect, from either parent or members of the extended family. For example, a child may overhear negative conversation or see negative emotions associated with the other parent, or be exposed to negative messages via emails, texts or social media. In other words, both parents' overt and covert behaviours need to support the script being provided to the child. This includes active measures to protect the child from being exposed to any past and/or ongoing conflict. For parents involved in long periods of acrimony and chronic litigation, this can be challenging when 'scripts' are firmly established. Equally, if parents have only just separated, negative feelings can be particularly intense and easily evoked. Furthermore, some parents have invested considerable time and energy in the narrative they hold and to relinquish it may come with a significant cost.

Components of coherent narratives

The key components of a coherent narrative constructed for children are as follows:

- Some degree of 'narrative continuity' (White & Epston 1990; Salvatore et al. 2004), matching the child's own current reality to some extent. It must not undermine the relationship with the closer parent; it validates, to some extent, negative feelings about the distanced parent even if facts are disputed

- Challenges to unsubstantiated allegations and extreme negative distortions of events. This is easier in cases where there has been a finding by the court indicating that one parent has negatively influenced the child against the other
- Represents each parent's reality so that it can be delivered in an authentic way without anxiety or pseudo-compliance. For example, a parent may dispute specific allegations of abuse, but is able to acknowledge and validate more broadly that there were times the child was very unhappy in their care, or scared by their behaviour
- Is simple and brief, focusing on general themes rather than too much detail. After all, the child will have the opportunity to ask questions, requiring the narrative to be elaborated on when this happens
- Is reparative of the relationship with the distanced parent, for example in the form of an apology to the child and/or between the parents
- Includes a statement that the parents, despite any previous or current disagreements, are now working together to promote the child's relationship with *both* of them.

The delivery of the narrative is most effective if:

- Space and time are allowed for the child to express his/her doubts and negative feelings and ask questions
- This is done consistently and authentically by both parents, both separately and jointly, and across other family/professional contexts
- It is not undermined, deliberately or inadvertently, by non-verbal communications by either parent and members of the wider family system
- It is developmentally appropriate and re-visited regularly and expanded over time.

Once a narrative has been constructed, some parents will need more coaching than others for its delivery. Parents may not feel able to provide and deliver the same narrative – and they may not wish to deliver it jointly and at the same time to their child(ren). Most children are used to hearing somewhat different accounts from their parents, and so two 'parallel' narratives are permissible as long as they do not disqualify or contradict each other, and, crucially, do not blame the other parent for the situation.

When parents are very preoccupied with the acrimony, it is necessary to literally rehearse scripts, for example focusing on the rationale for promoting contact and for reconnecting with the child following a long period of separation. Parents may need to be provided with strategies to manage their own affect and to anticipate and pre-empt difficult responses from the child. Mini role-plays are a helpful technique, which can stimulate more effective parental mentalizing, particularly when the parent takes on the role of the child and listens to the parental narrative told by the practitioner. Constructing and shaping narratives is not a one-off event and often much negotiation is involved. When parents are unable to agree and deliver a coherent narrative for their child, it may be left to the practitioner and/or other professionals to design and deliver it.

Aligning parental expectations and sustaining contact

It is not at all uncommon for distanced parents to quickly become impatient with the slow rate of progress which may be understandable given that they have already missed out on a huge amount of time, whereas the closer parent is frequently rather apprehensive about putting too much pressure on the child and progressing contact quickly. If, informed by the progress made, the parents can come to a shared agreement about the expected and desirable progression of contact fairly early on, then a potential source of conflict is removed and opens up a path to further progress. To calibrate their expectations about contact going forward both parents are required to put their child's needs at the centre of all decision making, including taking into account their child's different and changing developmental needs.

The goals established and agreed by both parents at the beginning of the work can be helpful in keeping the therapeutic intervention on track and identifying any barriers to progress early on. The general goal of work is almost always to protect the child(ren) from parental conflict and support their relationship with both parents. Parents can sometimes be further united in their goal to put an end to the conflict and progress with their lives. However, in cases of chronic litigation, it is not infrequently the case that contact work threatens to be terminated prematurely by at least one of the parents. This can happen for several reasons: the closer parent may only be prepared to engage in the minimum amount of interventions ordered by the court; the ongoing conflicts between the parents may prevent effective collaboration; and/or there may be financial constraints. Even in these cases children will usually have benefitted from having their unrealistic or distorted views of the distanced parent challenged. However, there is a risk that this relationship will not develop further or that old patterns of resisting contact will re-emerge – unless there is further work to ensure that contact is sustained, possibly with continuing pressure from the court.

In cases where therapeutic intervention has taken place relatively soon after contact difficulties or breakdown, work tends to progress more quickly. Parents' and children's positions are less polarized and there is usually less physical resistance from the child to attend contact, with agreeing on a narrative and re-establishing regular direct contact being less of a challenge.

Further work with the parental couple, wider family and professional network

Once some progress has been made, it can be sustained if meetings with the parental couple are scheduled in monthly intervals to review progress. Inter-parental communication and feedback systems can be set up, ideally via email, with the practitioner copied into any communications between the parents about issues concerning the children. Specific procedures can be established as to how frequent and voluminous the email contact should or can be and what the topics for inter-parental communication might be. The virtual presence of a third person – the practitioner – encourages many couples with a history of past email battles, to moderate their tone and any implied demands and criticisms. From time to time the practitioner may comment – via an email to both ex-partners – on specific aspects of the inter-parental email communications which should centre around handover, changes of contact schedules, plans regarding the child's birthday and festivals that need to be observed and/or celebrated and sometimes also about the introduction of a new partner or step-child. Inter-parental communication systems of this nature are a form of relapse prevention. To avoid parents becoming dependent on the practitioner for the facilitation of contact, responsible adults from the wider family and friendship network can be nominated to play an ongoing role in managing handover and supervising contacts, as well as helping parents to overcome communication difficulties and resolve disputes. Members of the child's wider family network who have been identified as potentially undermining contact can also be included in direct work at this stage, so as to help them recognize and understand the potential harmful impact on the child of their adversarial stance. Additional professional support may be sought and specific therapeutic interventions have been developed with the aim to increase the parental capacity to mentalize effectively, such as Mentalization-Based Family Therapy (Asen & Fonagy 2012b, 2017b; Keaveny et al. 2012), the Lighthouse Parenting Programme (http:lighthouseparenting.net) and Reflective Parenting (Cooper & Redfern 2015).

Relapse prevention and early recognition of unhelpful patterns

After several years of Mr M being separated from his children, the court ordered the reinstatement of contact between Josh, Ryan and Harry with their father. Contact took place on two occasions and Mr M was hopeful even though both children had remained totally silent and not made any eye contact with him. However, neither child had objected to attending contact and they also did not refuse to enter the room or run away crying, as they had done in the past. The children sat with their mother for around 20 minutes without saying a word. The subsequent scheduled contact session was cancelled by the mother, with no warning or explanation, leaving Mr M angry and fearful that the tenuous progress that he felt had been made would be lost. He responded by expressing his anger in a stream of irate emails to the children's mother. Ms M experienced this as harassment and she responded via her solicitor, asking Mr M to stop the messages and threatening that she would obtain a restraining order. Mr M felt misunderstood and denigrated and he worked even harder to make his case, contacting the children's guardian, the practitioners and others in the family's joint social network, stating that the mother was obstructing contact. Ms M and the children then began to cite the father's behaviour as evidence that he had not changed and that there should therefore be no contact.

Once contact has been re-established, and the child and distanced parent's anxiety at the prospect of contact has been overcome, it is helpful for parents to step back and try to identify patterns of behaviour that may lead to a relapse in the future – to avoid matters spiralling out of control. Parents can be reminded that people can change and that one should not jump to conclusions merely on the basis of an ex-partner's past behaviour. Specific contingencies can be put in place for situations that might trigger problematic patterns of behaviour. For example, agreements can be made as to how and when to obtain explanations about cancelled or postponed contacts. It may be helpful to identify a trusted adult in each parent's social network who can negotiate on behalf of each parent. This can then help moderate each parent's responses and allow them to mentalize themselves, their child and the ex-partner more effectively.

Chapter 8

Ensuring safe and reflective practice

Safeguarding issues and organizational 'holding'

The term 'reflective practice' (Schön 1983) refers to the ability to critically think about one's clinical practice, one's actions, thoughts and feelings, so that continuous learning can take place, particularly when complex clinical work is carried out. Work with high-conflict parents can be rather stressful for practitioners, leading to 'cumulative anxiety, irritability and depression, intensified by physical fatigue and a sense of depletion' (Wallerstein 1997). Clear policies and procedures around safeguarding and consent issues need to be in place in order to protect family members as well as practitioners. Whilst practical guidelines are important, they are insufficient if not accompanied by self-reflective practice which recognizes the challenges these families pose to a practitioner's mentalizing capacity and employs specific techniques to manage these.

Professionals involved in supporting children and families generally have a safeguarding responsibility, which involves continuous risk assessment and management. However, additional specific safeguarding issues in high-conflict families relate to a) obtaining informed consent, b) possibly overriding the child's expressed wishes and feelings, and c) dealing with criticisms which can be made by parents with regard to the practitioner's work. Failure to consider these issues from the outset can lead to significant delay in the work, as well as serious stress experiences for parents, children and professionals, with the possibility of intra-family issues being re-enacted by the wider system, leading to further impasses. Undertaking this type of work as a member of an established team and/or organization can provide the necessary support which practitioners who work independently and single-handedly, may not have. Regular supervision and being members of special interest groups, as well as participating in relevant training events is very important for all practitioners, and especially for those who do not have the support of a team or organization.

Consent and conduct issues

Given the ambivalence many parents have about changing the 'status quo', it is important to seek and provide clarification about the aims of the work from the very beginning. Once agreement has been reached about the proposed work – which is usually around promoting the child's relationship with *both* their parents – it is advisable to get both parents to sign a consent form which should do the following:

1. Provide detailed information about the proposed work
2. Explain the rationale for the intervention
3. Outline the safeguarding framework around the intervention
4. Acknowledge that it is probable that the child(ren) will initially be distressed when contact with the distanced parent is re-introduced and/or increased.

Both parents can be asked to identify potential barriers to progress and under what circumstances the work might be paused or terminated. For example, a closer father who may be rather ambivalent about whether contact is in his son's best interest, may later complain that his son was 'forced' to see his mother. However, if his ambivalence is explicitly identified as a barrier to change from the outset, the father can either decide to withdraw from the work (these cases may go/return to court) or take a different position in relation to contact, which is to fully support it, despite his son's protests. He cannot simultaneously hold this position and complain that his son was 'forced' to have contact.

It is important to communicate clearly at the outset of the work that it is the parent's – and not the practitioner's – responsibility to manage the child both physically and emotionally and to keep the child safe. This includes the closer parent also reassuring the child that he/she supports the contact with the distanced parent. Closer parents often communicate messages of support on one level, but non-verbally contradict these at the same time. Examples of seeming 'double messages' are provided in Box 8.1. When such double messages are directly observed, the practitioner can bring these to the parent's attention, though preferably not when the child is present.

Box 8.1 Examples of 'double message' interactions between a closer parent and child

- The child's seemingly distressed behaviour around contact leads to the parent becoming distressed in ways which are very visible to the child and further increase the child's distress.
- The parent does not directly challenge the child's dismissive and hostile behaviours towards the distanced parent.
- The parent tells the child to have contact with the distanced parent, but at the same time asks the child about his/her preferences or bargains with the child (e.g. 'Do you want to sit at the table with your mother or rather with me?'; 'If you go and see your father, we can go and do something really nice afterwards'; 'It's not me who says you need to see your mother, it is the court').
- The parent verbally supports contact, but non-verbally communicates to the child that it is an unpleasant or dangerous situation by, for example, looking very anxious and worried, or by providing endless and excessive reassurance, or by physically holding onto the child whilst stating that 'you must see your father'.
- The parent continually looks to the practitioner for guidance, telling the child repeatedly that 'I want you to see your father', but appealing to the practitioner 'What shall I say now?' when the child protests, thereby communicating that it is the practitioner's and not the closer parent's task to make contact happen and for it to be successful.
- The parent appears to support contact during the contact session, but recruits other adults – friends, GP, social worker, teacher – afterwards to build a case that further contact work is harmful to the child.
- The parent interacts with the distanced parent in hostile ways during contact handovers whilst claiming that it is 'important that you see your mother, you need to see her, otherwise I get into trouble'.

There are some circumstances when a child may initiate physical contact. This includes, for example, shaking hands and playing games where physical contact may be unavoidable, like football. There are other situations when the practitioner may feel the need to initiate physical contact with a child – above all in situations of perceived physical risk to a child, for example when a parent is acting aggressively. Distressed children may throw objects or kick furniture, destroy property or be physically abusive to the distanced parent and to the practitioner. On occasion a child may run out of the building into a busy street, with the parent refusing to follow the child and ensure his/her safety. This may leave no option for the practitioner other than to follow the child and ensure his/her safety, including using physical means of containment. This is where working in an organization that has a clear policy for when physical contact and means of containment can be employed, is particularly helpful.

It is not at all uncommon that when a child is presenting with challenging behaviours, the closer parent attempts to defer to the practitioner to manage the child, or emphasize, in the child's presence, that his/her reaction is understandable and constitutes evidence of how abusive the distanced parent has behaved in the past and how 'traumatic' the prospect of contact with that parent is. In cases where it is likely that a child will act out before or during direct contact with the distanced parent, it is important to ensure that discussions take place with the closer parent before any contact with the distanced parent starts, in order to consider how to manage a child's possible distressing behaviour and consider various strategies that the closer parent may need to adopt. In these cases it is essential to have two practitioners present as the situation can become very heated. Co-working also protects practitioners in the event that a parent misperceives the practitioner's intentions or actions and subsequently makes spurious and unfounded allegations, for example that the practitioner had restrained the child or otherwise prevented them from leaving the consulting room. Guidelines specifically tailored to this type of work need to be in place, clarifying and reinforcing boundaries and ensuring appropriate safeguarding of children. For example, a guideline might state that practitioners never initiate any physical contact with a child. However, if a child actively seeks physical contact with the practitioner by, for example, taking the practitioner's hand or clinging to the practitioner, the child's need is recognized verbally and gently re-directed to their responsible parent or carer. This helps to avoid any subsequent claims that the practitioner did physically coerce the child to have contact with the distanced parent. Careful documentation and strict record-keeping is essential when undertaking this form of work, if only to counter any possible allegations of misconduct that might be made against the practitioners.

When a child absolutely refuses to enter the room in which the distanced parent waits for contact, this should trigger an agreed set of actions from the practitioner and both parents. These are discussed, agreed and possibly even rehearsed with each parent separately via role plays prior to contact. This preparation will generally include ways in which the closer parent can encourage the child by explaining in an appropriate manner the rationale for contact, reassuring the child of their safety and expressing calmly and succinctly what is expected of the child. Role plays with the distanced parent may focus on a number of hypothetical scenarios, such as the child being totally silent, rude or physically attacking the parent, and possible responses are considered and rehearsed.

'Traumatic' contact

A particularly difficult dilemma for practitioners arises when the closer parent – and sometimes allied professionals – ask to terminate the contact work altogether because of the child's seemingly distressed behaviours. When considering the pros and cons of continuing with further contacts, it is important to think about the impact on the child's day-to-day life. This can lead to possibly adjusting the frequency of contact sessions in order to protect the stability of the child's home and school routines as much as possible, a difficult balancing act which has to be under continuous review. For example, a child aged 14 who is reported by school to be withdrawn and disengaged the day before and after contact may have less frequent contact with the distanced parent initially, in order not to adversely affect schooling. For a younger child, aged seven for example, there is less likely to be a long-term impact on their education but a considerable advantage of working more intensively to enable the child to make progress in forming and sustaining better relationships with both parents.

There are also circumstances when face-to-face contact with a previously abusive parent can re-traumatize a child. However, the risk of likely re-traumatization can be assessed and minimized during contact sessions by putting in place close supervision and appropriate preparation. At any rate, it is generally agreed that contact work should only take place if it is explicitly agreed by all that a) contact is in the child's best interest, and b) any resistance to contact the child displays is disproportionate to any negative experiences the child might have had in the distanced parent's care.

There are cases of parents initially agreeing to fully commit them-selves to the proposed assessment and subsequent therapeutic inter-ventions, but then becoming less enthusiastic or even actively sabotaging any further work. Here contact between the child and dis-tanced parent may need to be paused temporarily while each parent's commitment is ascertained. The practitioners may provide a brief report, detailing the barriers to change and, if there are legal proceed-ings, the report can be used to inform the court. Contact work is then not continued unless the obstacles to progress have been identified and addressed, and an explanation is provided to the child by the practitioner, with both parents' consent, so that any progress can be protected and in order to avoid the child feeling responsible for the impasse. An example of such explanation is reproduced in Box 8.2.

Box 8.2 Sample letter to the child

Dear John,

Thank you for coming with your mum to see us and your dad. We have seen some big changes here – to start off with you got very upset to even hear your dad's name and you had forgotten any-thing good that happened with him. With your mum and dad's help you have remembered some of the happier times, like when you all looked at the photos from Disneyland. Your dad has also heard what you said about how sometimes he used to shout at home and how this upset you. He told you how sorry he was about this, he realizes now that it was wrong. Your mum and dad have helped you to realize that you don't need to be scared of your dad, and you have seen for yourself that he is not cross about you not seeing him. We think it is very important for you to carry on seeing your dad, but we have noticed that sometimes, because your mum and dad have a very difficult relationship, your mum gets upset when she brings you to see dad – even though she tries not to. We have noticed that, understandably, this makes you feel upset, and so it makes it difficult to spend time with dad, because you and your mum are upset. We have suggested that one solution might be that your nan brings you instead, and your mum and dad and nan are going to think about this. When they have decided we will start the contact again.

Complaints

It is not uncommon for high-conflict parents involved in chronic litigation to make informal or formal complaints about professionals, be that practitioners, social workers, solicitors or even judges. For some parents litigation appears to have become almost a way of life. Obviously families receiving a clinical service have a right to complain if they are concerned about the quality of care they are receiving, and there should be a means for all families, including high-conflict parents, to do so. However, all too often the complaints made by parents and children in these situations tend to mirror the stuck and entrenched family dynamics: allegations are made against the practitioner for allegedly siding with one parent or they concern the treatment process, triggering complex and time-consuming administrative processes to manage the complaint. This tends to lead to delays, as clinical work may need to be suspended whilst the complaint is being formally investigated. Apart from slowing down or altogether preventing further work from taking place, considerable stress can be caused for the practitioners. As to the affected children, they have another emotionally abusive, fragmented experience, being initially re-introduced to a distanced parent who then literally disappears again as the work is paused and the complaint responded to. Complaints of this nature are usually brought by the closer parent, but can also be made by the distanced parent, for example, if there is disagreement about how fast the contact schedule should proceed. The intervention process then becomes the focus of conflict.

The process of responding to the complaint often includes the provision of detailed clinical records and correspondence, which are then scrutinized and can form the basis of further complaints. This costly and time-consuming process mirrors the 'chronic litigation' which has come to characterize some of these families. Investigations usually conclude that the complaint is unfounded. This is sometimes followed by a few further rounds of complaining about how the complaint has been handled – until the complaint procedures of an institution have been exhausted, usually to the parents' great dissatisfaction. Complaints may then be escalated, involving the practitioner's professional organization. Defamatory postings may be placed on the Internet. A sound safeguarding framework can help protect the work from being sabotaged by formal complaints while simultaneously protecting the rights of families to make complaints. When a case is in the court arena, any complaints about the process and direction of the work are probably most appropriately dealt with by the court. However, even with these safeguards in place, the lodging of formal complaints can represent a serious challenge to the progress of therapeutic work in these cases.

Some parents resort to making secret – i.e. non-consensual – audio-recordings of assessment and contact sessions, often with the aim of 'proving' that the practitioner was biased, disrespectful or bullying. Other parents may place recording devices on their children – during contact sessions with the other parent or to have a record of what their children say when being assessed by the practitioner, sometimes with and other times without the knowledge of the child. When asked to explain why they felt the need to record a session secretly, parents often reply that they feel their words have been 'twisted' or 'taken out of context', or that professionals deliberately 'lie' about what has been said in sessions. When parents explicitly ask whether they are permitted to record sessions, it is up to the practitioner to make a decision about whether this is appropriate or not. In the event that the practitioner agrees, one has to be mindful that audio-recordings – and particularly those which involve the parent's partner, may be shared with others and without obtaining every recorded person's informed consent. This then constitutes a serious breach of confidentiality, particularly when the audio-recordings are played to lawyers, family members or friends in an effort to demonstrate how 'evil' or 'silly' the other parent is.

Co-working

Given the complex dynamics found in most high-conflict families involved in entrenched legal disputes, it is advisable to co-work such cases. The co-working relationship provides a context for mutual reflection – before, during and after sessions – and allows the exploration of difference, disagreements and healthy challenges when appropriate. It is not at all uncommon for a practitioner, perhaps due to their own life experiences or cultural identity, to identify more strongly with one parent than with the other. Careful unpicking and understanding of such dynamics enables more effective practice. In addition, given the ease with which a practitioner's mentalizing capacity can go 'offline' when working with high-conflict cases, the presence of another mind can help by, for example, shifting the focus of attention back onto the child. Another context for self-reflective practice is provided via independent supervision and team meetings, permitting the consideration of alternative perspectives and interventions.

Frequency and length of time spent engaged in case-based reflective discussions will depend on the complexity of the work and other factors and it may vary from 5 minutes to 1 hour. A framework for co-working is provided in Table 8.1.

Table 8.1 A framework for co-working

What?	Who with?	How often?
De-brief	Co-worker	After every session if possible
Case review	Co-worker	Every 1–2 weeks
Case review/specific dilemma/issue discussed	Team (ideally MDT)	Every 2–3 weeks, or more regularly if required
Individual supervision	Clinical supervisor	Dependent on practitioner's level of experience (minimum monthly)

Chapter 9

Early interventions – avoiding litigation and court

Trial or controlled separation?

Separation is a major step for everyone, taking its toll with emotions alternating between grief and relief, sadness and anger, shock and denial. Children generally want to live with both their parents under the same roof – unless the inter-parental arguments have persisted for a very long time. The process of moving forward and accepting and adjusting to the new life tends to be slow for all concerned – and above all for children. Immediate decisions about practical issues such as finances can often be difficult and many disagreements will often surface. Professional help may be accessed, often in parallel rather than jointly.

When a marriage or other form of long-term relationship breaks down and parents eventually separate, children typically enter into new living arrangements with each parent. Whilst most separating parents begin to live in different dwellings, some do in fact continue to inhabit the same house for economic reasons. There are also those parents who choose 'nesting' in order to minimize the upheaval for their children – they may each stay with a friend or member of the family and rotate, moving in and out of the family home with the children staying put. If parents cannot agree on family life after separation – and this is more often than not the case in high-conflict families – lawyers and courts get drawn in and therapists and other professionals enter the scene. This is usually very costly, both in financial and emotional terms. Avoiding litigation and court is therefore an important consideration for all separating parents.

There are a number of options to manage separation and divorce without too much expense. Many couples will first agree on a period of informal separation before the separation becomes 'official' and can then have specific legal implications. When parents first consider a trial separation they do so to improve their relationship and to protect their children from the fallout of a permanent separation. Creating a temporary distance can assist in gaining new perspectives and it is often a helpful strategy to keep the family together in the long term. However, this scenario works best when well-defined separation agreements are made, covering issues such as childcare, contact between the children and both parents, the division of finances, assets and property. Parents can generally do this by themselves before seeking the assistance of a solicitor. When these arrangements are put in writing, they can be referred to during the course of any eventual divorce proceedings. Solicitor negotiation is another, costlier option and it consists of both parties' solicitors engaging in a process of correspondence and discussion to broker a solution on behalf of their respective clients without going to court. Sometimes collaborative law negotiations are conducted face to face in four-way meetings between the parties and their lawyers. Mediation is yet another option – here the parents try to resolve issues relating to their separation with the assistance of a professional family mediator. Mediation is frequently seen as the preferred means of resolving family disputes. In England, for example, any party wishing to make a court application following family breakdown is required to first attend a mediation information and assessment meeting (MIAM). In many European and North American countries mediation information sessions are recommended and in some countries they are compulsory, in the hope that agreements can be reached, above all in relation to dependent children. Judicial separation is a legal process without the finality of a divorce and is frequently chosen because of family and/ or cultural pressures or religious reasons. The parents remain legally married but can get court orders regarding their finances and childcare arrangements. It can be a cooling down period during which conciliation and/or counselling can happen.

Developing a shared 'mantra': protecting children's relationships with both their parents

Many separated parents are well aware of the importance of their children preserving a relationship with both their parents and they make this an absolute priority. However, entrenched conflicts between parents and the intense and complex feelings generated can lead to some parents losing sight of this priority. This is especially the case in families where one or both parents have themselves been bought up in the absence of one of their own parents, and/or where there is a strong family narrative around surviving in the absence of one parent. Sometimes there is also a culture within a family of other parental figures who, it is thought, are well able to fulfil the role of the absent parent. It is of course the case that many children thrive in one-parent families and benefit from the input of extended family and family friends. However, this does not ameliorate the harmful impact of being caught up in parental conflicts, which results in losing touch, physically and psychologically, with one of the previously loved parents.

If parents are at the point of separating they may wish to access some help in the form of parental couple counselling or therapy. This may help them to understand how their own experiences of being parented may be different from the parenting their children need. For example, parents who have themselves been emotionally and physically abused by one of their parents may benefit from reflecting on how this may have organized their own views about family life and parenting. Their own frightening representations of the abusive parent may be paired with guilt about having actively rejected that parent and can motivate parents to protect their child's relationship with both parents. In other cases, the demonization of an estranged mother in a father's childhood may lead him to repeat the 'family script' of bringing up children by fathers to the exclusion of mothers – without being consciously aware of it. If separated parents seek out psychological help in the form of parental couple counselling, it can help them to examine family scripts as well as how one's own experiences as a child can influence the making and shaping of relationships, including those with one's own children. Parental couple counselling does not mean that both parents need to attend at the same time; this can often seem too much of a challenge, particularly when emotions run high and the separation has been characterized by much acrimony.

Establishing a shared mantra from the very beginning of the process of parental separation to which both parents commit themselves explicitly, can help to protect the good intentions almost all parents have: 'We will aim to protect our children's relationship with both of us, whatever the level of conflict between us'. This involves also committing to the below principles:

- We will try to protect our children from direct exposure to the conflict between us (including disputes about contact and residence) and take care that they are not exposed to it vicariously, for example by witnessing our own critical or negative feelings about the other parent, or by having to overhear critical conversations or seeing posts on social media.
- We will provide our child with a consistent and coherent narrative about why we have separated, which does not attribute blame to the other parent and includes explicit reassurances that our children's relationship with each parent is separate from the relationship their parents have with each other.
- We will aim to provide our children with a consistent experience of being parented by devising and sticking to a written parenting agreement and reviewing this at agreed intervals.
- If, despite our best efforts, there are times when we do not achieve these aims, we will raise any concerns with the other parent immediately, either directly or via a mutually agreed third party.
- We will not question our children directly or indirectly (for example, by asking for detailed accounts) around the other parent's commitment to these principles.

Protecting the mantra

It is not usually difficult for well-intentioned parents to commit to these principles when first separating, but it can be a challenge to uphold them at times of intense conflict and when emotions surrounding relationship breakdown run high. Feelings of loss and grief, anger and betrayal, shame and disappointment can be accompanied by anxieties triggered by the process of adjustment to a different life and uncertainty about the future. The main challenge most parents face is protecting their children from exposure to these feelings, and separating these feelings from those that their children are experiencing. For example, a parent's experiences of anger or anxiety can feel so overwhelming that they are projected onto the child: 'My child is very angry' or 'My child is very anxious'. As we are all naturally disposed to try and make sense of the world, meaning then gets assigned to these feelings: 'She is angry because her mother ignored her' or 'He is anxious because he is scared of his father'. When this is communicated from one parent to the other, there is a risk that harmful triangulation processes emerge. For example, the level of contact is reduced unilaterally by a closer parent because they perceive their child to be anxious; this can lead the distanced parent to become angry which, in turn, the child picks up.

Parents can take certain measures to prevent this process from happening by:

- Proactively supporting contact
- Devising written parenting agreements
- Involving the wider family networks
- Strengthening and coordinating specific parenting skills
- Identifying and addressing problematic co-parenting patterns early on
- Agreeing on a coherent narrative for their children.

Proactive support of contact

Throughout this book we have stressed the importance of children having good and meaningful relationships with both parents. While strict 50:50 shared parenting might generally seem a fair way to ensure that this can happen, in practice it is rarely the case that children post-separation will spend identical amounts of time in the home of each parent. Young children in particular become tearful and clingy when they are separated from their familiar surroundings and their main primary carer, no matter whether this is the father or mother. This can be anticipated if the parents are able to work together and organize smooth transitions from one home to the other – and able to involve the other parent if and when separation anxieties flare up. Proactively thinking about what it is going to be like for the child to be in the care of the other parent can go a long way in preventing disappointments which sometimes take the form of the non-resident parent feeling not 'good enough' and then blaming the other parent for undermining their relationship with their child.

Most teenagers tend to go through several ups and downs for a few years, mediated by hormones, family dynamics and social encounters outside the family. They can be unpredictable and form a strong alliance with one parent against the other one week only to 'switch sides' a few days later. Predicting erratic behaviours, which include idealization of one parent and vilification of the other, which is then reversed in quick succession, will help parents not to feel too injured or rejected. Above all they will have to resist the temptation to use the temporary and fluctuating re-positioning of their adolescent children as ammunition for inter-parental battles.

Parenting agreements

Parents are often able to write these themselves, but in high-conflict separation scenarios they usually need help, which can be obtained via parental couple counselling/therapy. Each parent is asked to make a list of all the other important things they need to agree on in order to give their child a more consistent and coordinated experience of care. This exercise is beneficial in itself, because it demands that the parents consider their shared parenting from the child's perspective. For younger children, issues such as the bedtime routine may be important; for older children, rules and boundaries about, for example, going out with friends and phone use/ screen time, are more relevant. Parents are encouraged to think about why consistency is important for their child's well-being. Making this agreement explicit by writing it down reduces the chance that one parent will use a relaxation of the boundaries to gain the child's approval. Parents can come up with very long lists of issues to be agreed on and it is often necessary for the practitioner to help them to focus and prioritize a few key issues to begin with. Where there is more than one child, each child's individual needs must be considered. Mediators often engage in a similar process with separated parents, though usually with a different focus on, for example, financial arrangements. These are usually not discussed in parental couple counselling/therapy. Where the support of a mediator has been used previously, any arrangement made can be used as a starting point for a parenting agreement. Agreements can be revised: for example, an improvement in the quality of the relationship a child has with the non-resident parent may lead to a revision of the frequency and duration of contact. One primary task for the practitioner is to help parents to be realistic about their own and the other parent's limitations and the fact that it is not possible for them to control the other parent's behaviour. For example, if one parent is frequently late, and this is an established pattern, it is unlikely that they will suddenly become punctual at handover. To focus on punctuality is likely to be unfruitful and to lead to feelings of stress and disappointment on the part of the other parent. Instead this parent can be helped to think about what they can do to minimize the impact of the likely late arrival on the child, including managing their own expectations. Similarly, the other parent can be encouraged to think about how they know that lateness is an issue that causes stress for their ex-partner, and so, for the sake of their child(ren), instead of getting into battles about specific timings, make an effort to be punctual. Parenting agreements need to be reviewed in line with the child's changing developmental needs. A template including some key issues is provided in Box 9.1.

Box 9.1 Template for parenting agreements

Parenting agreement for:
Date of agreement:
Agreed date to review:

1) Proposed residence/contact arrangements

Type, frequency, duration and place of contact; handover arrangements

2) Responsibility for decision making

School and education, participation in leisure activities, medical issues, religious observance, planning holidays, location of/access to the child's passport

3) Communication content

Information sharing about school, travel, medical issues. Focus on the child and parenting issues. Ban on communicating about each parent's personal relationships. Ban on talking about the other parent in negative ways, both in the presence of the child or in ways that can be witnessed indirectly by the child (e.g. social media, via parental friends)

4) Communication method

Mode, timing and frequency of communications.
Trusted third party involvement over contentious/inflammatory issues

5) Dispute resolution

When and how to involve a trusted third party

6) Rules, routines and boundaries

Around daily parenting tasks, and including use of social media, child's mode of communication with non-resident parent

7) Consequences for breaking the rules

Including rewards/consequences/methods of discipline and withdrawal of privileges

Signatures:

Involving the wider family networks

Social support is key in helping each parent to manage their complex feelings and doubts and cope with the stress of parental separation. The ability to talk to a trusted family member or friend can generate different perspectives and disentangle parents' own feelings and experiences from those of their children. Furthermore, family networks can mediate between the parents when there are disagreements. A focus on restoring communities for children and separated parents (Van Lawick 2016) takes the mantra of protecting children from inter-parental conflict and supporting relationships with both parents a bit further: it is not only the loss of one of the parents which children in high-conflict families suffer – often those aligned with each parent, be that family or friends, take sides and refuse to have a relationship with the 'other' parent, compounding the child's losses and fragmentation.

Strengthening and coordinating specific parenting skills

When one parent has had little hands-on experience of child care, it is understandable that the other parent feels anxious about them caring for the child for extended periods of time. It may also be unrealistic to expect the inexperienced parent to be able to provide the same quality of child care and parenting skills their child is used to without considerable help and support. Acknowledging this and taking appropriate action can help reduce anxieties all round and provide the child with consistency and better quality care. Parenting agreements can be helpful here, particularly when there is a detailed description of important rules and boundaries. A member of the wider family network may be called upon to provide temporary support while the parent 'learns the ropes', for example how to manage a toddler's temper tantrum by using mutually approved strategies and keeping agreed boundaries in place. Sometimes referrals for a parenting course may be helpful.

Identifying and addressing problematic co-parenting patterns early on

It is somewhat obvious that the sooner one addresses problematic parenting patterns, the more likely it is that they can be resolved. Parental couple counselling/therapy can be helpful in identifying these patterns – whether those are based on genuine misunderstandings, on what children relay that the other parent has allegedly said or done, or on other third-party information.

Three distinct post-separation co-parenting styles have been described by Macoby and Mnookin (1992). *Cooperative parenting* involves the parents coordinating rules in the two households and supporting each parent's ongoing contact with their children, with relatively low levels of inter-parental conflict. *Conflicted co-parenting* is characterized by acrimony and disputes about how much time the child should spend with each parent, with repeated mutual accusations of maltreating the children, undermining contact and ignoring court orders. In *disengaged co-parenting* there is some form of parallel parenting, with each parent altogether avoiding contact with the other and with no coordination between the parents with regard to implementing rules. Recognizing a parental tendency towards problematic co-parenting as a result of primarily conflicted or disengaged parenting can be helpful in identifying patterns early on. However, these styles are not mutually exclusive.

Agreeing a coherent narrative for the children

The principles of constructing age-appropriate, coherent narratives for children have already been outlined in Chapter 7. At an early stage of the separation process it is important for children to get explanations from their parents, ideally delivered together, on the following points:

- That they are separating and why, with no blame attached to either parent
- That the child is not responsible for the parents' separation or any possible or likely reconciliation
- That the child's relationship with each parent is separate to the relationship their parents have with each other.

It is essential that parents immediately provide their children with clear and concrete reassurances regarding the practical arrangements around living between two homes. When there are concerns about a child's emotional reaction to the parental separation and its sequelae, parents may consider whether the child will need therapy in their own right. This is not an easy decision to make, as there are advantages and disadvantages of children having their own therapeutic space. An advantage may be that a 'neutral' space, away from the inter-parental battleground, allows the child to be able to talk about their innermost feelings, loyalty conflicts, fears and hopes, some of which they may not want to disclose to one or either parent. A disadvantage of referring children to a child psychotherapist is that there is a risk that they confide in, and begin to trust, someone else more than their own parents. The confidentiality rules of formal psychotherapy may keep the parents 'in the dark' as to the internal struggles their child is involved in. This is bridged by some psychotherapists who, adopting a systemic approach, will gradually bring one or both parents into the therapy sessions, after having discussed in some detail with the child which of their worries and concerns can be shared with one or both parents (Asen 2000).

Multi-family group approaches

In the midst of personal conflict and distress, most people find it difficult to be open-minded, let alone 'objective', about their own situation, yet they may well be able to be sensitive and thoughtful about the problems of other people. This phenomenon can be utilized in work with a group of six to eight families who are all struggling with similar issues, which permits mutual sharing and understanding, going beyond their own perspectives. In multi-family work (Asen & Scholz 2010), they are encouraged to help other families by observing and understanding seemingly identical problems and by making suggestions. Often one sees oneself 'reflected' – or mirrored – in others and family members begin to closely observe each other and to comment on what they like – or dislike – in others even if their own difficulties are identical. An eight-session family group programme, 'No Kids in the Middle', developed in the Netherlands by Van Lawick & Visser (2015), has shown much promise for dealing with high-conflict parenting. The main principles are: keeping the child in mind at all times, the inclusion of the family's networks, role plays and creative presentation ceremonies. This approach allows children to witness their parents working together in a safe space where the parents are able to focus on their children – and only on their children. It allows them to rediscover their qualities as parents who can empathize with their children's predicament. Doing so requires parents to shift from what has been termed 'parallel solo parenthood' (Cottyn 2009) to shared parenting attitudes and positions. However, the intervention is not recommended for families who have recently separated, recognizing that there is a need for time, post-separation, for the dust to settle and agreements to be reached. Families referred to the group are still experiencing high levels of conflict more than a year after separation.

Outlook

High-conflict separated parents can severely test any practitioner's capacity to maintain a mentalizing stance. The often extreme and polarized positions of each parent and their determination to convince the practitioner that only their version of events is correct and true, are very challenging. Even when Findings of Fact have been made by the court which totally contradict a parent's narrative, the seemingly unshakable conviction with which the narrative continues to be held can temporarily cause practitioners to question their own reasoning processes. When practitioners attempt to construct their own version of what happened, they can experience considerable feelings of anxiety, triggered by the cognitive dissonance arising out of the parents' credible but conflicting accounts. This can lead practitioners to feel just as triangulated as the child, with intense feelings of confusion and, at times, even annoyance. This parallel process represents only a diluted version of the distress usually experienced by children: they face the further challenge of having to connect their parents' different accounts with their own lived experiences which may well differ from both parents' accounts, whilst trying to maintain a trusting relationship with at least one of their parents.

Transference phenomena – such as a parent or child relating to the practitioner as if they were a parental figure, judge, social worker, policeman, teacher or grandparent – can also shape the practitioner's counter-transferential responses (Wallerstein 1997). There are, for example, situations when a practitioner may actually behave as if they are a judge or the benign grandparent the child never had. There may be times when the practitioner feels like an abusive parent who is forcing the child to do something against their wishes. There are occasions when the practitioner's own feelings of empathy towards a seemingly wronged parent may be very strong, making it hard to keep firm boundaries in place, potentially destabilizing the working relationship with the other parent. Practitioners may feel overwhelmed by a child's distress during contact with the distanced parent and feel compelled to cut it short. On other occasions, practitioners can be at risk of becoming firmly aligned with the distanced parent when the closer parent is not taking any responsibility for facilitating contact.

Making appropriate progress often creates an additional pressure for practitioners as they are charged with the responsibility for restoring a relationship between a child and a distanced parent – even when parents are unable or unwilling to stop the cycle of conflict. Limited progress can leave the practitioner feeling like they have failed. It is essential to be realistic about what is achievable and to be able to recognize and celebrate small successes if burnout is to be avoided. Counter-transferential phenomena put a considerable amount of pressure on the practitioner – they require team support, intervision and supervision in order to manage intense and conflicting feelings and keep their own mentalizing capacity 'online' in the course of undertaking this challenging work. Work with high-conflict parents can be both rewarding and stressful.

Such challenges mean that specialist intervention is scarce and hard for families and professionals to access in time to ameliorate or at least minimize harm to the child. Furthermore, because the negative impact of being triangulated may not be immediately evident in the child, the need for intervention may be missed. Yet, specialist intervention is desperately required as research has documented that the repeated and ongoing exposure of children to their separated parents' conflicts puts the children's mental health and long-term life chances at risk (Harold et al. 2016).

The concepts and interventions detailed in the body of this book may help practitioners to overcome and manage some of the inherent difficulties of working with this group by conceptualizing and formulating a child's resistance to contact and helping families, networks and professionals to move away from polarized positions of blame. Attachment and mentalizing frameworks assist the understanding of, and therapeutic response to, the seemingly irrational and hostile interactions between family members and their networks and the focus on systemic theory throughout promotes intervention that is context congruent and thus more likely to be effective and sustainable.

Finally, practitioners must never forget that the main work focus has to be on the welfare of the affected children – despite many parents' pleas to focus on them as the 'real victims'. The Family Ties approach aims to free children from the restraining ties imposed on them by parents and other members of the family and help them develop healthy ties and attachments with the significant people in their lives.

References

Abelin, E. (1975) Some further observations and comments on the earliest role of the father. *International Journal of Psycho-Analysis*, 56, 293–302.

Achenbach, T. M. & Edelbrock, C. (1991) *Child Behavior Checklist*. Burlington, VT: University of Vermont Press.

Ackerman, N. W. (1967) *Treating the Troubled Family*. New York: Basic Books.

Ainsworth, M. D. & Bell, S. M. (1970) Attachment, exploration, and separation: Illustrated by the behavior of one-year-olds in a strange situation. *Child Development*, 41, 49–67.

Ainsworth, M. D. S., Blehar, M. C., Waters, E. & Wall, S. (1978) *Patterns of Attachment: A Psychological Study of the Strange Situation*. Oxford: Erlbaum.

Amato, P. & Afifi, T. D. (2006) Feeling caught between parents: Adult children's relations with parents and subjective well-being. *Journal of Marriage and the Family*, 68, 222–236.

Amato, P. R. & Rezac, S. J. (1994) Contact with non-resident parents, interparental conflict, and children's behavior. *Journal of Family Issues*, 15, 191–207.

Anderson, H. & Goolishian, H. (1992) The client is the expert: A not-knowing approach to therapy. In S. McNamee & K. Gergen (eds.), *Therapy as Social Construction*. London: Sage Publications, Inc.

Andre, K. (2004) Parental alienation syndrome. *Annals of American Psychotherapy Association*, 7, 4–7.

Asen, E. (2000) Working with families where there is parenting breakdown. In P. Reder, M. McClure & A. Jolley (eds.), *Family Matters* (pp. 25–39). London: Routledge.

Asen, E. (2004) Collaborating in promiscuous swamps – the systemic practitioner as context chameleon? *Journal of Family Therapy*, 26, 280–285.

Asen, E. (2006) Assessing parents considered to pose serious risks to their children: The Marlborough approach. *Nyas*, 18, 178–188.

Asen, E. (2007) Therapeutic assessments: Assessing the ability to change. In C. Thorpe & J. Trowell (eds.), *Re-rooted Lives: Interdisciplinary Work with the Family Justice System* (pp. 39–47). Bristol: Jordan Publications.

Asen, E. (2010) entrenched parental positions post-separation – do they amount to a mental health disorder and how can they be treated? In M. Thorpe & M. Faggionato (eds.), *Mental Health and Family Law* (pp. 129–135). Bristol: Jordan Publications.

Asen, E. & Fonagy, P. (2012a) Mentalization-based therapeutic interventions for families. *Journal of Family Therapy*, 34, 347–370.

Asen, E. & Fonagy, P. (2012b) Mentalization-based family therapy. In A. Bateman & P. Fonagy (eds.), *Handbook of Mentalizing in Mental Health Practice* (pp. 107–128). Washington and London: American Psychiatric Publications.

Asen, E. & Fonagy, P. (2017a) Mentalizing family violence part 1: Conceptual framework. *Family Process*, 56, 6–21.

Asen, E. & Fonagy, P. (2017b) Mentalizing family violence part 2: Techniques and interventions. *Family Process*, 56, 22–44.

Asen, E. & Morris, E. (2016) Making contact happen in chronic litigation cases: A mentalizing approach. *Family Law*, 46, 511–515.

Asen, E. & Scholz, M. (2010) *Multi-Family Therapy: Concepts and Techniques.* London: Routledge.

Asen, E. & Schuff, H. (2003) Disturbed parents and disturbed families: Assessment and treatment issues. In M. Goepfert, J. Webster & M. V. Seeman (eds.), *Disturbed and Mentally Ill Parents and Their Children* (pp. 139–157). Cambridge: Cambridge University Press.

Aspland, H. & Gardner, F. (2003) Observational measures of parent–child interaction: An introductory review. *Child and Adolescent Mental Health*, 8, 136–143.

Bagby, R. M., Nicholson, R. A., Buis, T., Radovanovic, H. & Fidler, B. J. (1999) Defensive responding on the MMPI-2 in family custody and access evaluations. *Psychological Assessment*, 11(1), 24.

Baker, A. J. L. (2007) *Adult Children of Parental Alienation Syndrome: Breaking the Ties that Bind.* New York: W.W. Norton.

Baker, A. J. L. & Chambers, J. (2011) Adult recall of childhood exposure to parental conflict: Unpacking the black box of parental alienation. *Journal of Divorce and Remarriage*, 52, 55–76.

Baker, A. J. L. & Darnall, D. (2006) Behaviors and strategies employed in parental alienation: A survey of parental experiences. *Journal of Divorce & Remarriage*, 45, 97–124.

Baker, A. J. L., Gottlieb, L. K. & Verrochio, M. C. (2016) The reality of parental alienation: Commentary on 'judicial decision-making in family law proceedings' by Clemente, Padilla-Racero, Gandboy-Crego, Reig-Botella and Gonzalez-Rodriguez. *American Journal of Family Therapy*, 44, 46–51.

Baker, A. J. L. & Sauber, S. R. (eds.) (2013) *Working with Alienated Children and Families: A Clinical Guidebook.* London and New York: Routledge.

Bala, N. & Hebert, P. (2016) Children resisting contact: What's a lawyer to do? *Canadian Family Law Quarterly*, 36, 1–55.

Barletta, J. & O'Mara, B. (2006) A review of the impact of marital conflict on child adjustment. *Australian Journal of Guidance and Counselling*, 16, 91–105.

Barnard, K. E. & Kelly, J. F. (1990) Assessment of parent-child interaction. In S. J. Meisels & J. P. Shonkoff (eds.), *Handbook of Early Childhood Intervention* (pp. 278–302). New York: Cambridge University Press.

Barwick, H., Gray, A. & Macky, R. (2003) *Characteristics Associated with the Early Identification of Complex Family Court Custody Cases*. Wellington: Department of the Courts.

Bateman, A. & Fonagy, P. (2012) *Handbook of Mentalizing in Mental Health Practice*. Washington and London: American Psychiatric Publishing.

Bathurst, K., Gottfried, A. W. & Gottfried, A. E. (1997) Normative data for the MMPI-2 in child custody litigation. *Psychological Assessment*, 9(3), 205.

Beck, A. T. & Steer, R. (1988) Beck anxiety inventory (BAI). *BiB 2010*, 54.

Beck, A. T., Steer, R. A. & Brown, G. K. (1996) Beck depression inventory-II. *San Antonio*, 78, 490–498.

Beck, J. S., Beck, A. T. & Jolly, J. B. (2001) *Beck Youth Inventories of Emotional & Social Impairment: Depression Inventory for Youth, Anxiety Inventory for Youth, Anger Inventory for Youth, Disruptive Behavior Inventory for Youth, Self-concept Inventory for Youth: Manual*. Psychological Corporation.

Ben-Ami, N. & Baker, A. J. L. (2012) The long-term correlates of childhood exposure to parental alienation on adult self-sufficiency and well-being. *American Journal of Family Therapy*, 40, 169–183.

Bernet, W., von Bach-Galhau, A., Baker, A. & Morrison, S. L. (2010) Parental alienation DSM-V and ICD-11. *American Journal of Family Therapy*, 38, 76–187.

Bernet, W., Wamboldt, M. Z. & Narrow, W. E. (2016) Child affected by parental distress. *Journal of the American Academy of Child and Adolescent Psychiatry*, 55, 571–579.

Bing, E. (1970) The conjoint family drawing. *Family Process*, 9, 173–194.

Blow, K. & Daniel, G. (2002) Post-divorce processes and contact disputes. *Journal of Family Therapy*, 24, 85–103.

Bolgar, R., Zweeig-Frank, H. & Paris, J. (1995) Childhood antecedents of interpersonal problems in young children and adult children of divorce. *Journal of the Academy of Child and Adolescent Psychiatry*, 34, 143–150.

Boszormenyi-Nagy, I. & Spark, G. M. (1973) *Invisible Loyalties: Reciprocity in Intergenerational Family Therapy*. New York: Harper Row.

Bowen, M. (1966) The use of family theory in clinical practice. *Comprehensive Psychiatry*, 7, 345–374.

Bowen, M. (1978) *Family Therapy in Clinical Practice*. New York: Jason Aronson.

Bowlby, J. (1953) *Child Care and the Growth of Maternal Love*. London: Penguin.

Bowlby, J. (1969/1982) *Attachment and Loss. Vol. 1. Attachment*. New York: Basic Books.

Bream, V. & Buchanan, A. (2003) Distress among children whose separated or divorced parents cannot agree arrangements for them. *British Journal of Social Work*, 33, 227–238.

Bretherton, I. (1987) New perspectives on attachment relations: Security, communication, and internal working models. In J. D. Osofsky (ed.), *Wiley Series on Personality Processes. Handbook of Infant Development* (pp. 1061–1100). Oxford: John Wiley & Sons.

Brewin, C. et al. (2017) A review of current evidence regarding the ICD-11 proposals for diagnosing PTSD and complex PTSD. *Clinical Psychology Review*, 58, 1–15.

Brown, T. (2008) An Evaluation of a new post-separation and divorce parenting program. *Family Matters*, 78, 44–51.

Bruck, M. & Ceci, S. J. (1999) The suggestibility of children's memory. *Annual Review of Psychology*, 50, 419–439.

Buchanan, C. & Heiges, K. (2001) When conflict continues after the marriage ends: Effects of post-divorce conflict on children. In J. Grych & F. Fincham (eds.), *Interparental Conflict and Child Development* (pp. 337–362). New York: Cambridge University Press.

Budd, K. S. (2001) Assessing parenting competence in child protection cases: A clinical practice model. *Clinical Child and Family Psychology Review*, 4, 1–18.

Burns, R. C. & Harvard Kaufman, S. (1970) *Kinetic Family Drawings (K-F-D): An Introduction to Understanding Children through Kinetic Drawings*. New York: Bruner/Mazel.

Byng-Hall, J. (1986) Family scripts: A concept which can bridge child psychotherapy and family therapy thinking. *Journal of Child Psychotherapy*, 12, 3–13.

Byng-Hall, J. (1995) *Rewriting Family Scripts: Improvisation and Systems Change*. New York: Guilford Press.

Byrne, J. G., O'Connor, T. G., Marvin, R. S. & Whelan, W. F. (2005) Practitioner review: The contribution of attachment theory to child custody assessments. *Journal of Child Psychology and Psychiatry*, 46, 115–127.

Cantwell, B. (2018) New perspectives on the alienation of children following conflictual parental separation? *Seen and Heard*, 28, 61–65.

Cassell, D. & Coleman, R. (1995) Parents with psychiatric problems. In P. Reder & C. Lucey (eds.), *Assessment of Parenting: Psychiatric and Psychological Contributions* (pp. 169–181). London: Routledge.

Cecchin, G. (1987) Hypothesising, circularity and neutrality revisited: An invitation to curiosity. *Family Process*, 26, 405–413.

Ceci, S. J. & Bruck, M. (1993) The suggestibility of the child witness: A historical review and synthesis. *Psychological Bulletin*, 113, 403–439.

Chimera, C. (2018) What we man by parental alienation: Information for parents. *Context*, 157, 2–3.

Chorpita, B. F., Yim, L., Moffitt, C., Umemoto, L. A. & Francis, S. E. (2000) Assessment of symptoms of DSM-IV anxiety and depression in children:

A revised child anxiety and depression scale. *Behaviour Research and Therapy,* 38, 835–855.

Clawar, S. S. & Rivlin, B. V. (1991) *Children Held Hostage: Dealing with Programmed and Brainwashed Children.* Washington, DC: American Bar Association Section of Family Law.

Cleaver, H., Unell, I. & Aldgate, J. (1999) *Children's Needs-parenting Capacity: The Impact of Parental Mental Illness, Problem Alcohol and Drug Use, and Domestic Violence on Children's Development.* London: Stationery Office.

Connolly, M., Crichton-Hill, Y. & Ward, T. (eds.) (2006) *Culture and Child Protection.* London and Philadelphia: Jessica Kingsley Publishers.

Cooper, A. & Redfern, S. (2015) *Reflective Parenting: A Guide to Understanding What's Going on in Your Child's Mind.* London and New York: Routledge.

Cottyn, L. (2009) Conflicten tussen ouders na scheiding. *Systeemtheoretisch Bulletin,* 27, 131–161.

Crossman, A. M., Powell, M. B., Principe, G. F. & Ceci, S. J. (2002) Child testimony in custody cases: A review. *Journal of Forensic Psychology Practice,* 2, 1–32.

Cummings, E. M. & Davies, P. (2002) Effects of marital conflict on children: Recent advances and emerging themes in process oriented research. *Journal of Child Psychology and Psychiatry,* 243, 31–63.

Darnall, D. (1998) *Divorce Casualties: Protecting Your Children from Parental Alienation.* Lanham, MD: Taylor Publishing Co.

Davies, P. & Cummings, E. M. (1994) Marital conflict and child adjustment: An emotional security hypothesis. *Psychological Bulletin,* 116, 387–411.

DeJong, M. & Davies, H. (2012) Contact refusal by children following acrimonious separation: Therapeutic approaches with children and parents. *Clinical Child Psychology and Psychiatry,* 18, 185–198.

DiPasquale, L. (2000) The Marschak interaction method. In E. Munns (ed.), *Theraplay: Innovations in Attachment-Enhancing Play Therapy* (pp. 27–51). Plymouth: J. Aronson.

Drozd, L. M. & Williams Olesen, N. (2004) Is it abuse, alienation, and/or estrangement? *Journal of Child Custody,* 1, 65–106.

DSM-5. (2013) *Diagnostic and Statistical Manual of Mental Disorders,* 5th edition. Arlington: American Psychiatric Association.

Duncan, S. & Reder, P. (2000) Children's experience of major psychiatric disorder in their parent: And overview. In P. Reder, M. McClure & A. Jollry (eds.), *Family Matters: Interfaces between Child and Adult Mental Health* (pp. 83–95). London: Routledge.

Emery, R. E. (1982) Interparental conflict and the children of discord and divorce. *Psychological Bulletin,* 92, 310–330.

Ensink, K., Leroux, A., Normandin, L., Biberdzic, M. & Fonagy, P. (2017) Assessing reflective parenting in interaction with school-aged children. *Journal of Personality Assessment,* 99, 585–595.

Everett, C. (2006) Family therapy for parental alienation syndrome: Understanding the interlocking pathologies. In R. Gardner, R. Sauber & D. Lorandos (eds.), *International Handbook of Parental Alienation Syndrome* (pp. 228–241). Springfield, IL: Charles C Thomas.

Falkov, A. (1998) *Crossing Bridges: Training Resources for Working with Mentally Ill Parents and Their Children, Reader-for Managers, Practitioners and Trainers*. Department of Health.

Farber, S. K. (2008) Dissociation, traumatic attachments, and self-harm: Eating disorders and self-mutilation. *Clinical Social Work Journal*, 36, 63–72.

Feinberg, R. & Greene, J. T. (1997) The intractable client: Guidelines for working with personality disorders in family law. *Family Court Review*, 35, 351–365.

Fidler, B. J. & Bala, N. (2010) Children resisting post-separation contact with a parent: Concepts, controversies, and conundrums. *Family Court Review*, 48, 10–47.

Fidler, B. J., Bala, N. & Saini, M. (2013) *Children Who Resist Post Separation Contact: A Differential Approach for Legal and Mental Health Professionals*. New York: Oxford University Press.

Fonagy, P., Gergely, G, Jurist, F. & Target, M. (2002) *Affect Regulation, Mentalization, and the Development of the Self*. New York: Other Press.

Fonagy, P., Steele, M., Steele, H., Moran, G. S. & Higgitt, A. C. (1991) The capacity for understanding mental states: The reflective self in parent and child and its significance for security of attachment. *Infant Mental Health Journal*, 12, 201–218.

Fonagy, P. & Target, M. (1997) Research on intensive psychotherapy with children and adolescents. *Child and Adolescent Psychiatric Clinics of North America*, 6, 39–51.

Friedlander, S. & Walters, M. G. (2010) When a child rejects a parent: Tailoring the intervention to fit the problem. *Family Court Review*, 48, 98–111.

Friedman, M. (2004) The so-called high-conflict couple: A closer look. *The American Journal of Family Therapy*, 32, 101–117.

Gabarino, J. (1978) The elusive 'crime' of emotional abuse. *Child Abuse and Neglect*, 2, 89–99.

Garber, B. D. (2011b) Parental alienation and the dynamics of the enmeshed parent-child dyad. *Family Court Review*, 49, 322–345.

Gardner, R. (1985) Recent trends in divorce and custody litigation. *Academy Forum*, 29, 3–7.

Gardner, R. A. (1998) *The Parental Alienation Syndrome and the Evaluation of Child Abuse Accusations*. Creskill, NJ: Creative Therapeutics.

Gardner, R. A. (2001) *Therapeutic Interventions for Children with Parental Alienation Syndrome*. Creskill, NJ: Creative Therapeutics.

Geddes, M. & Medway, J. (1977) The symbolic drawing of the family life space. *Family Process*, 16, 219–228.

George, C., West, M. & Pettem, O. (1999) The adult attachment projective: Disorganization of adult attachment at the level of representation. In J. Solomon &

C. George (eds.), *Attachment Disorganization* (pp. 318–346). New York: Guilford Press.

Gilmore, S. (2006) Contact/shared residence and child well-being: Research evidence and its implications for legal decision-making. *International Journal of Law, Policy and the Family*, 20, 344–365.

Glaser, D. (2002) Emotional abuse and neglect (psychological maltreatment): A conceptual framework. *Child Abuse & Neglect*, 26, 697–714.

Goepfert, M., Webster, J. & Seeman, M. (eds.) (2004) *Parental Psychiatric Disorder – Distressed Parents and Their Families*, 2nd edition. Cambridge: Cambridge University Press.

Goldberg, W. & Goldberg, L. (2013) Psychotherapy with targeted parents. In A. Baker & S. Sauber (eds.), *Working with Alienated Children and Families: A Clinical Guidebook* (pp. 108–128). London and New York: Routledge.

Goodman, R. (1997) The strengths and difficulties questionnaire: A research note. *Journal of Child Psychology and Psychiatry*, 38, 581–586.

Gorell Barnes, G. (2005) Narratives of attachment in post-divorce contact disputes: Developing an intersubjective understanding. In A. Vetere & E. Dowling (eds.), *Narrative Therapies with Children & Their Families*. London and New York: Routledge.

Gorell Barnes, G. (2017) *Staying Attached: Fathers and Children in Troubled Times*. London: Routledge.

Gottlieb, L. J. (2012) *The Parental Alienation Syndrome: A Family Therapy and Collaborative Systems Approach to Amelioration*. Springfield, IL: Charles C Thomas.

Gould, J. W. & Martindale, D. A. (2007) *The Art and Science of Child Custody Evaluations*. New York: Guilford Press.

Grych, J. & Fincham, F. (2001) *Inter-parental Conflict and Child Development*. New York: Cambridge University Press.

Haley, J. (1963) *Strategies of Psychotherapy*. New York: Gruner and Stratton.

Haley, J. (1967) Toward a theory of pathological systems. In G. H. Zuk & I. Boszormeny-Nagy (eds.), *Family Therapy and Disturbed Families*. Palo Alto: Science and Behavior Books.

Harlow, H. F. (1960) Primary affectional patterns in primates. *American Journal of Orthopsychiatry*, 30, 676–684.

Harold, G., Acquah, D., Sellers, R. & Chowdry, H. (eds.) (2016) What works to enhance inter-parental relationships and improve outcomes for children. University of Sussex, Department of Work and Pensions.

Harold, G. T., Aitken, J. J. & Shelton, K. H. (2007) Interparental conflict and children's academic attainment: A longitudinal analysis. *Journal of Child Psychology and Psychiatry*, 48, 1223–1232.

Harold, G. T. & Murch, M. (2005) Inter-parental conflict and children's adaptation to separation and divorce: Implications for family law. *Child and Family Law Quarterly*, 17, 185–205.

Harold, G. T. & Sellers, R. (2018) Annual research review: Interparental conflict and youth psychopathology: An evidence review and practice focused debate. *Journal of Child Psychology and Psychiatry*, 59, 374–402.

Hertzmann, L., Abse, S., Target, M., Glausius, K., Nyberg, V. & Lassri, D. (2017) Mentalisation-based therapy for parental conflict – Parenting together, an intervention for parents in entrenched post-separation disputes. *Psychoanalytic Psychotherapy*, 31, 95–217.

Hertzmann, L., Target, M., Hewison, D., Casey, P., Fearon, P. & Lassri, D. (2016) Mentalization-based therapy for parents in entrenched conflict: A random allocation feasibility study. *Psychotherapy*, 53, 388.

Hodges, J., Steele, M., Hillman, S., Henderson, K. & Kaniuk, J. (2003) Changes in attachment representations over the first year of adoptive placement: Narratives of maltreated children. *Clinical Child Psychology and Psychiatry*, 8, 315–367.

Holmes, M. R. (2013) The sleeper effect of intimate partner violence exposure: Long-term consequences on young children's aggressive behaviour. *Journal of Child Psychology and Psychiatry*, 54, 986–995.

Holt, S., Buckley, H. & Whelan, S. (2008) The impact of exposure to domestic violence on children and young people: A review of the literature. *Child Abuse & Neglect*, 32, 797–810.

Hunt, J. & Trinder, L. (2011) Chronically litigated contact cases. How many are there and what works. *Family Law*, 41, 1375–1378.

International Classification of Diseases – 11th Revision (ICD-11) (2018) https://icd.who.int/

Jenkins, J. M., Dunn, J., Rasbash, J., O'Connor, T. G. & Simpson, A. (2005) Mutual influence of marital conflict and children's behaviour problems: Shared and non-shared family risks. *Child Development*, 76, 24–39.

Johnston, J. R. (1993) Children of divorce who refuse visitation. In C. E. Depner & J. H. Bray (eds.), *Nonresidential Parenting: New Vistas in Family Living* (pp. 109–135). Thousand Oaks, CA: Sage Publications, Inc.

Johnston, J. & Goldman, J. (2010) Outcomes of family counseling interventions with children who resist visitation: An addendum to Friedlander and Walters (2010). *Family Court Review*, 48(1), 112–115.

Johnston, J. R., Gonzalez, R. & Campbell, L. E. (1987) Ongoing post-divorce conflict and child disturbance. *Journal of Abnormal Child Psychology*, 15, 497–509.

Judge, A. M. & Deutsch, R. M. (eds.) (2017) *Overcoming Parent-Child Contact Problems: Family-Based Interventions for Resistance, Rejection and Alienation*. New York: Oxford University Press.

Keaveny, E., Midgley, N., Asen, E., Bevington, D., Fearon, P., Fonagy, P., Jennings-Hobbs, R. & Wood, S. (2012) Minding the family mind: The development and initial evaluation of mentalization-based treatment for families. In N. Midgley & I. Vrouva (eds.), *Minding the Child* (pp. 98–112). Hove & New York: Routledge.

Kelly, J. (2007) Children's living arrangements following separation and divorce: Insights from empirical and clinical research. *Family Process*, 46, 35–52.

Kelly, J. B. & Emery, R. E. (2003b) Children's adjustment following divorce: Risk and resilience perspectives. *Family Relations*, 52, 352–362.

Kelly, J. B. & Johnston, J. R. (2001) The alienated child: A reformulation of parental alienation syndrome. *Family Court Review*, 39, 249–266.

Kelly, K., Slade, A. & Grienenberger, J. F. (2005) Maternal reflective functioning, mother–Infant affective communication, and infant attachment: Exploring the link between mental states and observed caregiving behavior in the intergenerational transmission of attachment. *Attachment & Human Development*, 7, 299–331.

Klein, M. (1946) Notes on some schizoid mechanisms. *The International Journal of Psychoanalysis*, 27, 99–110.

Kline, M., Johnston, J. & Tschann, J. (1991) The long shadow of marital conflict. *Journal of Marriage and the Family*, 53, 287–309.

Lebow, J. (2003) Integrative family therapy for disputes involving child custody and visitation. *Journal of Family Psychology*, 17, 181–192.

Lebow, J. & Rekart, K. (2007) Integrative family therapy for high-conflict divorce with disputes over child custody and visitation. *Family Process*, 46, 79–91.

Lilienfeld, S. O., Lynn, S. J., Ruscio, J. & Beyerstein, B. L. (2010) A remembrance of things past: Myths about memory. In S. O. Lilienfeld, D. J. Lynn, J. Ruscio & B. L. Beyerstein (eds.), *50 Great Myths of Popular Psychology: Shattering Widespread Misconceptions about Human Behaviour*. UK: Wiley-Blackwell.

Lindaman, S. L., Booth, P. B. & Chambers, C. L. (2000) Assessing parent–child interactions with the Marschak Interaction Method (MIM). In K. Gitlin-Weiner, A. Sandgrund & C. Schaefer (eds.), *Play Diagnosis and Assessment* (pp. 371–400). Hoboken, NJ: John Wiley & Sons.

Loftus, E. (1997) Creating false memories. *Scientific American*, 277, 70–75.

Lowenstein, L. (2006) The psychological effects and treatment of the parental alienationsyndrome. In R. Gardner, R. Sauber & D. Lorandos (eds.), *International Handbook of Parental Alienation Syndrome* (pp. 286–291). Springfield, IL: Charles C Thomas.

Lowenstein, L. (2007) *Parental Alienation*. Lyme Regis: Russell Publishing House.

Lowenstein, L. F. (1998) Parent alienation syndrome: A two step approach toward a solution. *Contemporary Family Therapy*, 20, 505–520.

Luyten, P. et al. (2009) *The Parental Reflective Functioning Questionnaire-1 (PRFQ-1)*. Leuven, Belgium: University of Leuven.

Macoby, E. E. & Mnookin, R.H. (1992) *Dividing the Child: Social and Legal Dilemmas of Custody*. Cambridge, MA: Harvard University Press.

Main, M., Kaplan, N. & Cassidy, J. (1985) Security in infancy, childhood and adulthood: A move to the level of representation. In I. Bretherton & E. Water (eds.), *Growing Points in Attachment Theory and Research*, Monographs of the Society for Research in Child Development, Serial No. 209, 50 (pp. 66–104). Chicago: University of Chicago Press.

Major, J. (2006) Helping clients deal with parental alienation syndrome. In R. Gardner, R. Sauber & D. Lorandos (eds.), *International Handbook of Parental Alienation Syndrome* (pp. 286–291). Springfield, IL: Charles C Thomas.

McIntosh, J. E. (2001) Thought in the face of violence: A child's need. *Child Abuse & Neglect*, 26, 229–241.

McIntosh, J. E. (2003) Enduring conflict in parental separation: Pathways of impact on child development. *Journal of Family Studies*, 9, 63–80.

Millon, T. & Bloom, C. (2008) *The Millon Inventories: A Practitioner's Guide to Personalized Clinical Assessment*, 2nd edition. New York: Guilford Press.

Minuchin, S. (1974) *Families and Family Therapy*. London: Tavistock.

Morris, E. & Asen, E. (2018) Developing coherent narratives for children of high-conflict parents. *Context*, 157, 8–11.

Morrison, F. (2015) 'All over now?' The ongoing relational consequences of domestic abuse through children's contact arrangements. *Child Abuse Review*, 24, 274–284.

Neff, R. & Cooper, K. (2004) Parental conflict resolution: Six-, twelve-, and fifteen-month follow-ups of a high-conflict program. *Family Court Review*, 42, 99–114.

Novick, J. & Novick, K. (2005) Soul blindness: A child must be seen to be heard. In L. Gunsberg & P. Hymowitz (eds.), *A Handbook of Divorce and Custody* (pp. 81–90). Hillsdale, NJ: Analytic Press.

OECD (2018) www.oecd.org/els/family/SF_3_1_Marriage_and_divorce_rates.pdf

Pinnell, M. & Harold, G. (2008) Inter-parental conflict and psychological impacts on children: The development of a CAFCASS cymru risk assessment toolkit as an example of research into practice. *Seen and Heard*, 18, 21–28.

Rait, D. (2000) The therapeutic alliance in couples and family therapy. *Journal of Clinical Psychology*, 56, 211–224.

Raman, S. (2006) Cultural identity and child health. *Journal of Tropical Pediatrics*, 52, 231–234.

Rand, D. (2011) Parental alienation, critics and politics of science. *American Journal of Family Therapy*, 39, 48–71.

Reay, K. M. (2015) Family reflections: A promising therapeutic program designed to treat severely alienated children and their family system. *The American Journal of Family Therapy*, 43, 197–207.

Richardson, M. (2019) Parental alienation: The vital early stages of litigation. *Family Law*, 49, 278–285.

Roussow, T. (2012) Self-harm in young people: Is MBT the answer? In N. Midgley & I. Vrouva (eds.), *Minding the Child* (pp. 131–144). Hove and New York: Routledge.

Royal College of Psychiatrists (2016) *Parental Mental Illness: The Impact on Children and Adolescents*. Information for parents, carers and anyone who works with young people. Retrieved from: rcpsych.ac.uk/healthadvice/parent sandyouthinfo/parentscarers/parentalmentalillness.aspx

Rutter, M. & Quinton, D. (1984) Parental psychiatric disorder: Effects on children. *Psychological Medicine*, 14(4), 853–880.

Salvatore, G., Dimaggio, G. & Semerari, A. (2004) A model of narrative development: Implications for understanding psychopathology and guiding therapy. *Psychology and Psychotherapy*, 77(2), 231–254.

Schacter, D. L. (2001) *The Seven Sins of Memory: How the Mind Forgets and Remembers*. Boston, MA: Houghton Mifflin.

Scharp, K. M. & Dorrance Hall, E. (2017) Family marginalization, alienation, and estrangement: Questioning the nonvoluntary status of family relationships. *Annals of the International Communication Association*, 41, 28–45.

Schön, D. A. (1983) *The Reflective Practitioner: How Professionals Think in Action*. New York: Basic Books.

Seltzer, J. A. & Bianchi, S. M. (1988) Children's contact with absent parents. *Journal of Marriage and Family*, 50, 663–677.

Selvini Palazzoli, M., Boscolo, L., Cecchin, G. & Prata, G. (1980) Hypothesizing-circularity-neutrality, three guidelines for the conductor of the session. *Family Process*, 19, 3–12.

Selvini Palazzoli, M., Cirillo, S., Selvini, M. & Sorrentino, A. M. (1990) *Family Games: General Models of Psychotic Processes in the Family*. New York: W.W. Norton.

Sharp, C. & Fonagy, P. (2008) The parent's ability to treat the child as a psychological agent: Constructs, measures and implications for developmental pathology. *Social Development*, 17, 737–754.

Shmueli-Goetz, Y., Target, M., Fonagy, P. & Datta, A. (2004) The child attachment interview: A psychometric study of reliability and discriminant validity. *Developmental Psychology*, 44, 939–956.

Siegel, J. (1996) Traditional MMPI-2 validity indicators and initial presentation in custody evaluations. *American Journal of Forensic Psychology*, 13, 55–63.

Slade, A. (2005) Parental reflective functioning: An introduction. *Attachment and Human Development*, 7, 269–281.

Slade, A., Aber, J. L., Berger, B., Bresgi, I. & Kaplan, M. (2003) *The Parent Development Interview–Revised*. City University of New York: Unpublished manuscript.

Slade, A., Grienenberger, J., Bernbach, E., Levy, D. & Locker, A. (2005) Maternal reflective functioning, attachment and the transmission gap: A preliminary study. *Attachment and Human Development*, 7, 283–298.

Smith, M. (2004) Parental mental health: Disruptions to parenting and outcomes for children. *Child and Family Social Work*, 9, 3–11.

Smyth, B. M. & Ferro, A. (2002) When the difference is night and day: Parent-child contact after separation. *Family Matters*, 63, 54–59.

Solomon, J. & George, C. (2008) The measurement of attachment security and related constructs in infancy and early childhood. In J. Casidy & P. Shaver (eds.), *The Handbook of Attachment* (2nd edition, pp. 383–416). New York: Guilford.

Stern, D. (1985) *The Interpersonal World of the Infant: A View from Psychoanalysis and Development*. New York: Basic Books.

Stewart, R. (2001) *The Early Identification and Streaming of Cases of High Conflict Separation and Divorce: A Review*. Department of Justice Canada.

Sturge, C. & Glaser, D. (2000) Contact and domestic violence – The experts court report. *Family Law*, 30, 615–629.

Sullivan, M. J., Ward, P. A. & Deutsch, R. M. (2010) Overcoming barriers family camp: A program for high-conflict divorced families where a child is resisting contact with a parent. *Family Court Review*, 48, 116–135.

Target, M., Fonagy, P. & Shmueli-Goetz, Y. (2003) Attachment representations in school-age children: The development of the child attachment interview (CAI). *Journal of Child Psychotherapy*, 29, 171–186.

Tavris, C. & Aronson, E. (2007) *Mistakes Were Made (But Not by Me): Why We Justify Foolish Beliefs, Bad Decisions and Hurtful Acts*. Orlando, FL: Houghton Mifflin Harcourt.

Templer, K., Matthewson, M., Haines, J. & Cox, G. (2017) Recommendations for best practice in response to parental alienation: Findings from a systematic review. *Journal of Family Therapy*, 39, 103–122.

Toren, P., Bregman, B. L., Zohar-Reich, E., Ben-Amitay, G., Wolmer, L. & Laor, N. (2013) Sixteen-session group treatment for children and adolescents with parental alienation and their parents. *The American Journal of Family Therapy*, 41, 187–197.

Trinder, L., Kellet, J. & Swift, L. (2008) The relationship between contact and child adjustment in high conflict cases after divorce or separation. *Child & Adolescent Mental Health*, 13, 181–187.

Van Lawick, M. J. (2016) Restoring communities for children and separated parents. In I. McCarthy & G. Simon (eds.), *Systemic Therapy as Transformative Practice* (pp. 233–250). London: Everything Is Connected Press.

Van Lawick, M. J. & Visser, M. M. (2015) No kids in the middle. *Australian and New Zealand Journal of Family Therapy*, 36, 33–50.

Verrocchio, M. C., Baker, A. J. L. & Marchetti, D. (2018) Adult report of childhood exposure to parental alienation at different time periods. *Journal of Family Therapy*, 40, 602–618.

Vidair, H. & Rynn, M. (2010) *Childhood Anxiety Disorders: Best Treatment Options and Practice*. Cambridge, UK: Cambridge University Press.

Wallerstein, J. (1997) Transference and countertransference in clinical interventions with divorcing families. In M. Solomon & J. Siegel (eds.), *Countertransference in Couples Therapy* (pp. 113–124). New York: W. W. Norton.

Warshak, R. A. (2010) Family bridges: Using insights from social science to reconnect parents and alienated children. *Family Court Review*, 48, 48–80.

Watzlawick, P., Jackson, D. & Beavin, J. (1967) *Pragmatics of Human Communication*. New York: W.W. Norton.

Weir, K. (2011) Intractable contact disputes: The extreme unreliability of children's ascertainable wishes and feelings. *Family Court Review*, 49, 788–800.

Weitzman, J. (2013) Reunification and the one-way mirror. In A. Baker & S. Sauber (eds.), *Working with Alienated Children and Families: A Clinical Guidebook* (pp. 188–208). London: Routledge.

Westphal, S. K., Poortman, A.-R. & Van der Lippe, T. (2015) What about the grandparents? Children's postdivorce residence arrangements and contact with grandparents. *Journal of Marriage and Family*, 77, 424–440.

Whitcombe, S. (2017) Parental alienation or justified estrangement? Assessing a child's resistance to a parent in the UK. *Seen and Heard*, 27, 31–47.

White, J. (1999) *Overcoming Generalised Anxiety Disorder*. Oakland, CA: New Harbinger.

White, M. & Epston, D. (1990) *Narrative Means to Therapeutic Ends*. New York: W.W. Norton.

Woodall, K. & Woodall, N. (2017) *Understanding Parental Alienation: Learning to Cope, Helping to Heal*. Springfield, IL: Charles C Thomas.

Index

Made in the USA
Coppell, TX
22 March 2021